NAHC

# Wild Game Cookbook

*designed and edited by*

Jane Obern
Valarie Waldron

Published by the North American Hunting Club, Inc.
Minneapolis, MN 55435

We would like to thank the following for their help:

**Coleman,** for advice and helpful information on outdoor cooking.

**International Chili Society,** for their award-winning recipes.

**NAHC Approved Guides and Outfitters,** for giving us a great selection of their "tried and true" recipes.

**G.O.A.B.C.,** for cooking tips and camp recipes.

**Paula Del Giudice,** NAHC member and only registered female guide in Nevada, for her generous help.

**Remington,** for use of the cover photograph.

**Celebrities,** for letting us share their favorite game recipes.

**NAHC Members,** for their contributions to this "outdoor cooking" edition.

**Anthony Biscotti,** for the wildlife art.

Cover photo of "Remington Country" scene from Remington's 1986 catalog courtesy of Remington Arms Company, Inc., Wilmington, Delaware.

*Address reprint requests and orders for additional books to:*

NAHC Cookbook Editor
Post Office Box 35557
Minneapolis, MN 55435

# CONTENTS

Introduction . . . . . . . . . . . . . . . . . . . . . . . . . . . . . . . . . . . . .  4
   *by Paul S. Burke, Jr., Chairman of the Board*

Outdoor Cooking . . . . . . . . . . . . . . . . . . . . . . . . . . . . . . . .  7
   *A variety of ways to make tasty camp meals*

Home Cooking . . . . . . . . . . . . . . . . . . . . . . . . . . . . . . . . . 77
   *Bring your cooking back indoors*

Chili . . . . . . . . . . . . . . . . . . . . . . . . . . . . . . . . . . . . . . . . .117
   *International Chili Society gives us their best*

Celebrity Chefs . . . . . . . . . . . . . . . . . . . . . . . . . . . . . . . .161
   *Favorite recipes from industry leaders*

Send Us Your Recipes . . . . . . . . . . . . . . . . . . . . . . . . . . .185
   *We want to hear your wild game recipes*

Index . . . . . . . . . . . . . . . . . . . . . . . . . . . . . . . . . . . . . . . . .189

# COOKING IN THE GREAT OUTDOORS

You know it as well as I do. Even the best French chefs with their delicate sauces and flaming side dishes can't come up with a meal that tastes better than a plate of beans and fresh tenderloin served up over a crackling fire in hunting camp. It just doesn't get any better than that.

But there is one catch. Camp cooking can be a tricky skill to master. And no matter how beautiful the starlit night or how thrilling the distant cries of geese, bad chow just doesn't make for amiable campmates.

Paul S. Burke, Jr.

To make those nights in camp perfect for you and to keep your campmates content, the NAHC staff has pulled together the best outdoor cooking recipes from NAHC members, guides and outfitters whose food you rated as excellent in your hunting reports, and from the members of the Guides-Outfitters Association of British Columbia. Outdoor cooking is the focus of this NAHC Wild Game Cookbook.

All great cooks have one thing in common; they're not afraid to use their imagination. A recipe is nothing more than a starting point. You can add or subtract whatever you like to make it uniquely your own.

Unfortunately, the "sterile" environment of the kitchen often stifles the creative urge in outdoorsmen like us. The family likes a recipe prepared "by the book", so that's the way you fix it—period.

But outdoor cooking, be it on a gas camp stove, over a bed of glowing coals, or in a Dutch oven, is a whole new ball game.

There is no better time or place to let your imagination run wild! Whether it's finding a green stick to use as a spit, making an oven out of two pie tins, or brewing your coffee in an old tin can, success of outdoor cooking relies on the cook's imagination.

In the outdoor cooking section, you'll find several recipes you can prepare at home and take into camp with you. Besides tasting great, these offer advantages like ease of transport, preparation and clean-up. It is comforting to have meals in camp that can be prepared quickly when you come in tired, cold and wet!

Since before he learned to control it, fire has been a source of inspiration for man. Now, in the great outdoors, it can be your inspiration for wonderful and exciting new meals.

Of course, recipes for use in the convenience of your own kitchen haven't been neglected. As is now the custom for NAHC cookbooks, we've gathered the very best from you and your fellow NAHC members, hunting industry leaders, and this year even from the International Chili Society.

Enjoy these recipes in your hunting camp this fall and for years to come, but use caution! The meals will be so pleasing you're liable to get permanent K.P. duty.

Continued hunting success,

Paul S. Burke, Jr.
Chairman of the Board
North American Hunting Club

- Fresh meat will keep for several days if sealed in a jar and sunk underwater in a spring or creek.

- Salt moose steaks down in a crock, sprinkle each layer with a few drops of vinegar, put in a cool place and they will keep for several weeks.

- To tenderize wild meat or ducks, soak overnight in salt water and enough vinegar to just put a bit of sour taste to the water.

- If bacon molds, clean with a vinegar soaked cloth.

- Edible organs of game are highly perishable. Prepare and cook as soon as possible.

- Bear meat should be cooked until well done as there is a danger of trichinosis.

- When roasting a lean piece of meat, drying out can be prevented by fastening strips of fat around the meat with a string.

- Less tender meat is made tender and flavorful by long slow cooking in moist heat.

- A little bit of ground beef fat added to lean ground wild game is delicious.

- Use some instant potato powder or dehydrated mushroom soup to thicken a stew.

# YEAST BISCUITS

Yield: 10-12
Prep Time: 2 hours

1 cup lard
1 cup mashed potatoes
1 quart scalded milk
½ cup sugar
1 cake quick-rising yeast
  flour
2 tsp. salt
1 tsp. baking soda
2 tsp. baking powder

Mix lard, mashed potatoes and scalded milk. Let cool. Add sugar and yeast (dissolved in warm water), then flour (enough to make batter). Let rise, add salt, soda and baking powder. Beat batter thoroughly and add enough flour to make a biscuit dough. Let rise and cut into biscuits. Let rise again. Bake 10 minutes. These may be reheated.

G.O.A.B.C.

# CAMP BAKING POWDER BISCUITS

Yield: 36 biscuits
Prep Time: 30 minutes

- 12 **cups flour**
- 2 **T. salt**
- 4 **T. baking powder**
- 1 **cup shortening**
- 2 **cups dry milk**

Sift together flour, salt, baking powder. Cut in shortening.
Add dry milk and combine well. Store in zip-lock bags or other
air tight container. Approximately 45 minutes before serving
meal, place 2 cups of mix per every 6 biscuits in a bowl and
add ¾ to 1 cup water. Stir quickly until moistened. Turn out on
floured board (or flour the wax side of freezer wrap for easy
clean up). Knead a few times, then pat to ¾-inch thickness.
Cut biscuits with a can opened at both ends. Roll biscuits in
melted margarine and place on a baking sheet. Bake in hot
camp oven or at 375 degrees for 15 to 20 minutes or until
browned.

*Mary Beth Kibler*
Kibler Outfitter & Guide Service
Box A-6
Sand Springs, MT 59077

# DUTCH OVEN BISCUITS

Serves: 6-10
Prep Time: 20-30 minutes

Mix Bisquick according to directions for biscuits. Don't over stir the mix.

Take hot coals and set outside fire pit. Oil large Dutch oven inside thoroughly. Set the Dutch oven on the coals to heat for 10 minutes or so. Spoon the mixture into the Dutch oven. Cover the oven with lipped lid. Shovel hot coals onto the Dutch oven. Cook for 20-30 minutes, depending on how hot the coals are. Check after 20 minutes. The biscuits should be lightly browned.

*Paula Del Giudice*
Reno, Nevada

# DUTCH OVEN BISCUITS

Yield: 4
Prep Time: 20 minutes

| | |
|---|---|
| 2 cups flour | 4 T. shortening |
| ½ tsp. salt | 1 cup milk |
| 3 tsp. baking powder | |

Blend all dry ingredients together. Blend in shortening with a fork until mixture is crumbly. Add milk and stir until mixture sags by spoon indentation. Knead dough on floured surface for at least 30 seconds. Pull dough out to ½ inch thick. Cut with round cutter or form by hand. Put in greased Dutch oven, cover and bury in hot coals for 5 to 10 minutes or until golden brown.

*Jeff Wolaver*
Colorado Drop Camps
P.O. Box 38254
Colorado Springs, CO 80937

## BANNOCK

Yield: 6
Prep Time: 30 minutes

2½  cups flour
¼  cup skim milk powder
¾  cup water
2  T. egg powder
½  tsp. salt
2  tsp. baking powder
1  T. melted grease

or 1 cup milk
1-2 eggs

Sift dry ingredients together. Mix well. Add liquids and melted grease. Stir until flour is wet. Knead slightly. Place in greased pan or in cast iron pan. Cook until golden on both sides, approximately 20 minutes.

*Mayra Koivukoski*
Sioux Retreat Services
P.O. Box 1304
Sioux Lookout, Ontario POV 2TO

## CORN FRITTERS

Yield: 12
Prep Time: 15 minutes

1  cup flour
1  tsp. baking powder
¼  cup milk
1½  cup cooked kernel corn

1  tsp. salt
2  eggs
1  T. melted shortening

Mix wet and dry ingredients lightly. Heat Dutch oven and grease. Drop mixture from tablespoon into hot grease and fry for 4 to 5 minutes. Drain on paper towel.

G.O.A.B.C.

========== Camp Cooking ==========

## GOLDEN CORN BREAD

Yield: 16 squares
Prep Time: 25 minutes

| | |
|---|---|
| 2 eggs | 1 cup flour |
| 1 cup milk | 1 tsp. salt |
| ¼ cup melted shortening | 3 tsp. baking powder |
| ¾ cup yellow corn meal | 2 T. sugar |

Beat all ingredients until smooth. Bake in a wax paper lined 9-inch square pan at 400 degrees about 20 minutes.

*Margaret Copenhaver*
Copenhaver Outfitters
Box 111
Ovando, MT 59854

## BREAKFAST MUFFINS

Yield: 12
Prep Time: 20 minutes

| | |
|---|---|
| ½ cup sugar | 1 tsp. baking powder |
| ¼ cup melted margarine | 1 cup flour |
| 1 egg | ¼ cup melted margarine |
| ½ cup milk | ½ cup sugar, mixed with |
| ½ tsp. nutmeg | 1 tsp. cinnamon |

Mix all ingredients except last 3. Place in greased muffin tin and bake 15 to 20 minutes at 375 degrees. Turn out and dip in melted margarine and sugar/cinnamon mixture. Serve warm.

*Linda Baumeister*
Lone Wolf Guide Service
Box 631
Livingston, MT 59047

# Helpful Hints

- Turn pancakes when bubbles start breaking. They are done when soft to the touch.

- Hotcakes and eggs should be served off the griddle, never stacked up ahead of time.

- Stewed prunes, figs or applesauce can be served alternately with juice.

- Steaks, hamburgers, etc. can be served alternately with bacon.

- When making pancakes, make a little salt bag and rub the griddle with it instead of grease. The cakes will not stick and there will be no smoke or odor.

- When making pancakes on an aluminum griddle, do not grease your griddle, but add the melted shortening to your batter. Use fine steel wool for polishing your griddle.

- When making pancakes, rub the griddle with cut potatoes instead of using fat. It doesn't leave the house (or tent) filled with the odor of pancakes.

- Cook bacon in baking pan in the oven.

- A couple of hard boiled eggs and salt, left over roast ribs or fried chicken or grouse is a good substitute for a sandwich.

- Lunches should not be made the night before.

- A tea billy should be carried by each guide.

- When boiling cracked eggs, white vinegar added to the water will help keep the white from running out.

- Lunch boxes will be sweet smelling if a piece of fresh bread dampened with vinegar is left in them overnight.

=== Camp Cooking ===

## GINGERBREAD PUFFS

Yield: 12 puffs
Prep Time: 35 minutes

1 egg
1 cup sugar
¼ cup molasses
¼ cup salad oil
1 cup flour
⅛ tsp. salt

½ tsp. soda
½ tsp. ginger
¼ tsp. nutmeg
¼ tsp. cinnamon
½ cup boiling water

Combine egg, sugar, molasses and oil thoroughly. Add sifted dry ingredients; mix. Add water and mix. Fill greased muffin pans ⅔ full. Bake at 350 degrees for 25 to 30 minutes.

*Margaret Copenhaver*
Copenhaver Outfitters
Box 111
Ovando, MT 59854

## INDIAN PIE

Serves: 4-6
Prep Time: 45 minutes

| | |
|---|---|
| 6 cups flour | ¾ cup lard |
| 1 cup raisins | ½ tsp. salt |
| 3 tsp. baking powder | 2-3 cups water |

Mix flour, lard, baking powder, salt and raisins together. Add water to make dough. Make one big piece and flatten dough to about 1-inch thickness and put into a greased pan. Cook for about 20 to 30 minutes or until brown.

G.O.A.B.C.

## FRIED BREAD

Yield: 6
Prep Time: 25 minutes

| | |
|---|---|
| 3 cups flour | 3 tsp. baking powder |
| ¾ tsp. salt | 2 T. shortening |
| ⅓ cup powdered milk | warm water |

Mix all ingredients with warm water to make a soft dough. Form into small balls and let sit for 10 to 15 minutes. Preheat skillet with oil. Roll out dough into flat circles (or use hands to pat out), fry on both sides.

*Pat Jacobson*
Arctic Rivers Guide Service
Box 1313
Kodiak, AK 99615

# PEMMICAN

The best pemmican is made from dried, powdered meat. It can be used with lard, bear fat, caribou fat, goose fat or moose fat. Smoke the dried meat. Pound it and make a nice powder. Mix with water to form a batter. Some people like to add berries and sugar. In winter, put it outside to freeze and keep it frozen. In the summer, make it more like a dough and cover it. It keeps well for a long time. Pemmican is used especially in the winter by trappers when they walk all day and want to travel light. A piece the size of a date square is enough for a meal. It is good with a cup of tea.

G.O.A.B.C.

# ROAST BEEF OR PORK, PRECOOKED FOR PACKING

Place roast into oven, uncovered, and cook for 1-1½ hours in a 425-450 degree oven (or until brown on outside and red in center). Remove and wrap in cellophane. Put gravy/juice into a jar with a tight lid. At camp, slice meat and warm in a pan with butter. Put juice into pan and thicken with a can of mushroom soup or 1 heaping T. buttermilk hotcake mix.

Mushroom soup is good for thickening gravy of all fried meats. After removing meat, add a can of cream of mushroom soup to hot fat. Stir and add hot water or vegetable juice until desired thickness is reached.

Buttermilk hotcake mix can be used as thickening without mixing with water. It will not be lumpy. Just add 1 T. or more right in stew or gravy.

G.O.A.B.C.

# CAMP FIRE COOK-OUT

Serves: 4
Prep Time: 30 minutes

- 1 lb. ground meat
- 1 lb. onion
- 3 carrots
- 4 potatoes
  salt and pepper

Divide meat and make 4 large patties. Place patties, 1 each, on 4 sheets of heavy foil. Peel and slice vegetables and divide between patties. Season with salt and pepper. Wrap foil loosely around each individual serving, but tighly seal edges. Place on grill about 4 inches above medium fire. Cook 15 minutes, turn and cook about 15 minutes more or until vegetables are tender.

*Linda Baumeister*
Lone Wolf Guide Service
Box 631
Livingston, MT 59047

# GREG'S QUICK MEAL

Serves: 1
Prep Time: 8 minutes

| | |
|---|---|
| ½ lb. hamburger | ½ onion, diced |
| 1 carrot, diced | ¼ can peas |
| 1 potato, diced | salt and pepper |

Combine ingredients and mix well. Put in aluminum foil and cook 3 minutes each side in hot coals.

*Gregory Phillips*
Milwaukee, Wisconsin

# TRAIL HAMBURGER SANDWICH

Yield: 4-6
Prep Time: 1 hour

  1   **lb. ground meat**
  ½   **cup onions, chopped**
  ½   **cup cabbage, finely chopped**
  ½   **tsp. Worcestershire**
      **salt and pepper**

Prepare a yeast bun dough. While it is rising, prepare the hamburger filling. In heavy skillet, cook all ingredients. Set aside to cool. When bun dough has risen to double in bulk, punch down and turn out onto floured board. Roll to ¼-inch thickness. Cut into rounds about 4 inches across. On one round, put a spoonful of meat mixture to within ¼ inch of edge. Put another round on top and pinch edges together. Let rise until light and bake as regular buns. When cool, wrap well in foil. Can be placed on a grill or a rock by campfire to reheat. Also can be frozen to keep for a longer period of time.

G.O.A.B.C.

# HOBO STEW

Serves: 4
Prep Time: 2¼ hours

- 2 potatoes, sliced
- 1 cup onion, chopped
- ½ cup celery, chopped
- 1 can pork and beans
- 1 can tomato soup
  salt and pepper
- 1 lb. lean hamburger

Put potatoes, onion and celery in bottom of casserole. Salt and pepper. Put beans on top, then tomato soup. Cover with hamburger (uncooked). Bake for 2 hours at 350 degrees.

G.O.A.B.C.

# MIXED BAG SOUP

Serves: 4-6
Prep Time: 10½ hours

    1 lg. beef soup bone
      water to cover
      wings, carcass or legs of
        game animals or birds
    1 lg. onion, chopped
    3 ribs celery, chopped
    1 2-inch wedge of cabbage, chopped
    1 lg. tomato
    3 lg. carrots, chopped
    2 sm. potatoes, chopped
    1 cup peas
    1 cup lima beans
    1 cup string beans, cut
    1 cup corn

Place bone in large pan and cover with water. Add salt and pepper. Cover and simmer for 8 hours. Remove the bone and refrigerate broth until the fat congeals. Remove fat, add as many game parts as you wish, cover and simmer for 2 to 3 hours until all ingredients are tender. Strain broth, remove bones. Add onion, celery, cabbage, tomatoes, salt and pepper to taste. Cover and simmer until vegetables are done. Remove meat from cooled bones and cut into small pieces. Add carrots to broth, cook for 10 minutes then add rest of vegetables. Cook until tender, add meat and heat to serve.

*E. Jenkins*
Elkland, Pennsylvania

## SUSIE'S OGDENSBURG CAMPFIRE STEW

Serves: 4-6
Prep Time: 1½-2 hours

- 2 lbs. stew meat
- 4 potatoes
- 4 carrots
- 1 onion
  fresh mushrooms
  salt and pepper
  pinch of oregano
- 1 stick butter
- 2 T. parsley
- ½ can beer (old style)

Cut the meat, potatoes, carrots and onion in small cubes. Mix all ingredients together (except the butter). Put ½ cup of mixture in a piece of foil, put butter on top, close up tight and put on camp fire.

*Columbus Caldwell*
Waupaca, Wisconsin

# FRYPAN MACARONI MEAL

Serves: 6
Prep Time: 35 minutes

  2 T. oil
  ½ cup onion, chopped
  1 lb. ground game meat
3½ cups cooked tomatoes
  1 cup celery, diced
  ½ cup green pepper, chopped
  1 tsp. salt
  ⅛ tsp. pepper
  ½ tsp. celery salt
  1 tsp. Worcestershire
  ½ tsp. chili powder
  2 cups cooked macaroni
    chopped parsley
    grated cheese

Bring to a boil 4 cups salted water. Add 2 cups macaroni and cook according to directions. Preheat frypan, add oil, and fry onion until done. Add meat and brown. Add tomatoes, celery, green pepper and seasonings. Bring to a boil and simmer about 20 minutes. Add cooked macaroni, simmer 10 minutes more. Sprinkle with parsley and cheese.

*Howard Copenhaver*
Copenhaver Outfitters
Box 111
Ovando, MT 59854

## ONE POT MEAL

Serves: 2
Prep Time: ½ hour

   1 **small onion**
   ½ **lb. ground beef**
   2 **T. oil**
   1 **can vegetable soup**
     **spices**

Heat oil in pan; saute onion until golden brown. Add ground beef and brown. Drain off excess oil. Add the soup and heat thoroughly, approximately 5 to 7 minutes. Add any spices you like.

*Stephen Thompson*
East Berne, New York

## HAMBURGERS IN A CAN

Yield: 6-8
Prep Time: ½ hour

|   |   |
|---|---|
| 2 **lbs. ground beef** | 1 **tsp. salt** |
| 1½ **lb. ground pork** | 3 **drops Tabasco** |
| 1¾ **cup rolled oats** | **pepper** |
| 2 **eggs, beaten** | ½ **cup onions, minced** |
| 2 **T. mustard** | 1 **cup evaporated milk** |

Mix all ingredients and pack into 3 20-ounce cans, leaving 1 inch space at top. Cover tightly and freeze. To remove from cans, open bottom and push out. Slice and fry. To put on grill, wrap in foil.

G.O.A.B.C.

===== Camp Cooking =====

# MINESTRONE DINNER

Yield: 4
Prep Time: 3½ hours

- 3 lbs. cubed meat
- 2 T. salt
- ½ cup onions, diced
- 2 cups dry kidney beans
  water to cover
  vegetables: celery, cabbage, carrots, squash, peas,
             string beans, canned tomatoes, etc.
- 1 onion, minced
- 1 lb. ground meat
  salt and pepper
- 1½ cup broken spaghetti

Cook first 5 ingredients about 3 hours, adding more water when needed. Cool. Remove any bones and most of the fat. Saute onion, ground meat, salt and pepper, and add to first part, along with any longer-cooking vegetables. Simmer. Add spaghetti and quicker-cooking vegetables about 20 minutes before serving time. Use your own variations and quantities of vegetables and spices.

G.O.A.B.C.

## HOLUPCHI

Serves: 4
Prep Time: 1½ hours

| | |
|---|---|
| 1 medium cabbage | 1 onion |
| ¼ cup vinegar | salt and pepper |
| ½ lb. rice | 1 lg. can tomatoes |
| ¼ lb. bacon | |

Remove core from cabbage. Add ¼ cup vinegar to large pan of water, bring to a boil. Scald cabbage in water long enough to wilt leaves. Remove leaves and slice off heavy mid-rib, so that they won't break when rolled. Wash rice and boil hard for 10 minutes in salted water. Drain. Dice bacon fine and fry until crisp. Drain. Mix bacon, rice, salt and pepper. Spread a spoonful of mixture on each cabbage leaf and roll tightly. Line large baking dish with boiled cabbage leaves, place cabbage rolls close together on them and pile on top of one another until dish is full. Cover with more cabbage leaves. Pour on tomatoes and season. Bake at 375 degrees for 1½ hours, then cover and bake for ½ hour.

## BEAVER TAIL BEANS

Serves: 2-4
Prep Time: 45 minutes

Blister tail over fire until skin loosens (or dip into boiling water for a couple of minutes). Pull off skin. Cut up and boil with a pot of beans. Add salt and pepper to taste. Some chopped onions add to the flavor. Beaver tail is also good roasted over a campfire or in the oven.

G.O.A.B.C.

# CURRIED RICE AND MEAT

Yield: 6
Prep Time: 2 hours

| | |
|---|---|
| 4 onions, minced | 4 stalks celery |
| 1 T. oil | 1 cup peas |
| 3 lbs. meat, cubed | 1 cup tomatoes |
| 2 tsp. curry powder | 6 potatoes |
| 4 carrots | salt and pepper |

Saute onions in oil until tender. Add meat and cook about 10 minutes. Add curry powder, stir until well blended. Add carrots, celery, peas and tomatoes. Add 1 cup water and simmer slowly about an hour until everything is tender. Add potatoes and continue cooking about 40 minutes. Add salt and pepper to taste. Serve over rice.

*Pat Jacobson*
Arctic Rivers Guide Service
Box 1313
Kodiak, AK 99615

# JAVY WRAP-UPS

Serves: 2
Prep Time: 1 hour

- ½ lb. ground javelina
- 1 shot tequila
- 1 tsp. lime juice
- 1 clove garlic, minced
  salt and pepper
- 1 egg
- 2 tsp. bread crumbs
- 1 onion, sliced
- 1 potato, sliced

Mix all ingredients except onion and potato. Form into patties and freeze (for added flavor, refrigerate for 2 days before freezing). When in camp, lay potato slices and onion rings between patties and wrap in foil. Place in hot coals for about 2 or 3 hunting stories or until onions and potatoes are cooked.

*Andrew Wyly*
Tucson, Arizona

# SLOPPIES

Serves: varies
Prep Time: ½ hour

bacon
potatoes
onion

water
garlic salt
salt and pepper

Cut bacon slices into small pieces in bottom of iron frying pan.
Let simmer while slicing potatoes into pan. Slice 1 onion, add
to pan. Pour boiling water over all, not quite to top of potatoes.
Add a pinch of garlic salt, salt and pepper. Cover and cook
until potatoes are done.

G.O.A.B.C.

# CAMP JERKY

Serves: varies
Prep Time: at least 8 hours

Use the leftover scraps from boning out deer or elk. Cut meat
into strips 1-2" wide, 3-5" long and not more than ½ inch
thick. Sprinkle meat with salt, pepper, and garlic powder on
all sides.

Arrange meat to hang from a rack or tripod (at least 3 feet
above fire in the smoke) using wire or string hangers. Smoke
for at least 8 hours. Use a portable tripod, if possible, so you
can move the meat to stay in the direction the smoke is
blowing.

*Paula Del Giudice*
Reno, Nevada

1. Be clean while cooking.
2. Always wash hands before fixing food, even if it is just a cup of coffee.
3. Do not let your nose drip. Do not sniff. Use your handkerchief and wash hands later.
4. Don't scratch yourself.
5. Never comb your hair around the cooking area.
6. Do not smoke while cooking. Wash hands after smoking.
7. Keep aprons, dish towels and dish rags clean.
8. Keep a good supply of water in camp.
9. Rinse dishes well in a large panful of very hot water with 1 tablespoon bleach added.
10. Put pots away bottom side up.
11. Cover all dishes with a plastic cloth.
12. Wipe grease and spilled foods from your stove.
13. Never use fly-dope unless everything in the kitchen is covered.
14. Have screens on the windows and doors.
15. Keep your supplies neat.
16. Keep foods that will spoil in a cooler.
17. Don't use your hunting knife in the kitchen without washing it.
18. Keep your butcher knife sharp.
19. Do not put bacon where it is damp.
20. Taste prepared food to see if it is alright—but use a spoon, not your fingers.
21. Do not burn food.
22. Always make a good pot of coffee the first thing in the morning.
23. Be sure the breakfast plates are warm.
24. Always be cheerful.
25. Don't drink liquor on the job.

# CAMPFIRE TACOS

Serves: varies
Prep Time: ½ hour

**For each serving:**
**¼ pound deer or elk steak, ¾ inch thick**
**salt and pepper, to taste**
**chili powder, to taste**
**Beaumonde seasoning, to taste**
**garlic powder, to taste**
**onion powder, to taste**

**Garnishings, as desired:**
**onions, chopped**
**tomatoes, chopped**
**lettuce, chopped**
**peppers, chopped**
**salsa**
**sour cream**
**grated cheese**

**fresh flour tortillas**

On a hot griddle, grill both sides of tortillas quickly to warm.

Barbecue meat over medium coals on both sides until cooked to taste. Remove meat and slice thinly. Wrap meat in tortillas and add condiments as desired. Serve with refried beans and/or Spanish rice.

*Paula Del Giudice*
Reno, Nevada

# DUTCH OVEN STROGANOFF

Serves: 6-8
Prep Time: 1-2 hours

1½-2  **lbs. round steak**
  1  **onion, chopped**
    **oil**
    **garlic powder, to taste**
    **salt and pepper, to taste**
  2  **small cans mushrooms**
  2  **cans cream of mushroom soup**
  1  **8-oz. container sour cream**
    **noodles or rice**

Slice steak into thin strips approximately 2 inches long and ½ inch wide. Heat oil in Dutch oven and brown onion lightly. Add steak and brown on all sides. Add seasonings. Cover beef with water and simmer slowly for 1 to 2 hours. Add additional water, if necessary.

Stir in soup and mushrooms. Heat thoroughly. Just before serving, stir in sour cream and cook just until heated through. Serve over noodles or rice.

*Paula Del Giudice*
Reno, Nevada

# DUTCH OVEN ELK POT ROAST

Serves: 6
Prep Time: 2-2½ hours

| | |
|---|---|
| 3-4 lbs. elk roast | 6 carrots |
| 1 cup flour | 4 sticks celery |
| ½ tsp. pepper | 6 small potatoes |
| 1 tsp. salt | water to cover |
| 3 onions, quartered | |
| 1 clove garlic, mashed | |

Clean meat well. Mix flour, salt and pepper and rub onto roast. Have Dutch oven on coals and hot. Brown meat on both sides well. Cut vegetables and add to roast. Pour water over to cover. Cover and bury Dutch oven in coals. Renew coals half-way through cooking.

*Jeff Wolaver*
Colorado Drop Camps
P.O. Box 38254
Colorado Springs, CO 80937

# BARBEQUED ELK TERIYAKI STEAK

Serves: 6
Prep Time: 30 minutes

  2  **24-oz. elk sirloin steaks**
     **teriyaki sauce**
     **salt and pepper**
     **garlic salt**

Brush steaks generously with teriyaki sauce. Lightly add salt, pepper and garlic salt. Let marinate in sauce at least 1 hour. After marination, place steaks on barbeque grill over hot coals. Cook on both sides and remove from grill when steaks are about medium-rare. Slice steaks diagonally into thin strips. Do not over-cook steaks as they will cook some while slicing. This may be used as a French Dip.

*Kay Trogdon*
Lazy T4 Outfitters
P.O. Box 116
Victor, MT 59875

## EASY VENISON STEW

Serves: 6-8
Prep Time: 3-6 hours

  1½-2 lbs. hearty chunks of deer, trimmed
      salt and pepper
      Beaumonde seasoning, to taste
   ½ onion, chopped
   1 clove garlic, chopped
 3-4 potatoes, cut in large chunks
   2 16-ounce cans whole tomatoes
   4 stalks celery, sliced
   ½ cup mushrooms, fresh or canned, sliced

In a deep skillet or Dutch oven, heat oil and brown onion and
garlic. Add meat and brown lightly on all sides. Add remaining ingredients and cook slowly for 3 to 6 hours.

## EASY CHILI

Serves: 6-8
Prep Time: 2-3 hours

      1 onion, chopped
      1 clove garlic, chopped
      oil
  1½-2 lbs. deer or elk meat, cut into ½-inch chunks
      2 16-ounce cans whole tomatoes, undrained
  1 or 2 16-ounce cans pinto beans, drained
      red pepper, to taste
      1 tablespoon cumin
      salt and pepper, to taste

Heat oil. Brown onion and garlic lightly. Add meat and brown
on all sides. Add remaining ingredients and simmer for 2 to 3
hours.

*Paula Del Giudice*
Reno, Nevada

# POT ROAST

Serves: 8-10
Prep Time: 6-8 hours

- 4 lbs. deer or elk
  oil
- 1 clove garlic, minced
- 2 onions, chopped
- 3 medium potatoes
- 4 medium carrots
- 1 onion
- 1 carrot
- 1 stalk celery
- 1 can consomme
- ¼ cup Worcestershire

In large, deep skillet or Dutch oven, heat oil and brown garlic lightly. Cut meat into chunks and brown on all sides in hot oil. Take meat out of pot. Cube the vegetables and spread evenly over the bottom of the pot. Pour in one can consomme. Put meat on top of the vegetable mixture and season with salt and pepper to taste. Place the rest of the vegetables around the meat. Add 1 cup water and Worcestershire sauce. Cover. Set on edge of fire and cook slowly for 6-8 hours or, if using a Dutch oven bury the oven in a pit with coals.

*Paula Del Giudice*
Reno, Nevada

# CAMPFIRE POT ROAST

Serves: 6
Prep Time: over 2 hours

A large piece of meat makes a great meal in camp and is handy for sandwiches thereafter. Any cooking process which is self-basting is best for very fresh, lean meat. Season roast with salt and pepper and garlic. Sear it on all sides, combine 1 cup of apple juice/cider with about ¼ cup flour and pour this over. Put lid on, set pan in coals and let it bubble away. Length of cooking time varies form a couple of hours to longer. Toss in a handful of onion flakes or fresh onion, adding vegetables when nearly done.

# PIT-FIRE ROAST

Serves: 6
Prep Time: 6-8 hours

> **roast of venison, moose, caribou, etc.**
> **salt and pepper**
> **any other desired seasonings**

Keep a good fire going in a pit about 1 foot deep until it is full of red coals. Have at least 4 to 6 inches of red coals for your roasting. Prepare game roast with salt, pepper and any other seasonings you desire. Place in heavy foil and seal edges by crimping them together. Bank coals around roast cover all with sand and let roast for 6 to 8 hours. Remove sand carefully and use care also in opening foil. Save juices to serve over sliced meat.

*Pat Jacobson*
Arctic Rivers Guide Service
Box 1313
Kodiak, AK 99615

# CHUCK WAGON STEW

Serves: 4-6
Prep Time: 2 hours

    1  cup small dried white beans
    3  cups water
    5  slices bacon, diced
    3  large onions, chopped
    1  lb. lean ground meat
    1  1-lb. can tomatoes
    1  tsp. salt
    2  T. brown sugar
 1½  tsp. dry mustard

In large kettle, bring beans to a boil in water. Boil for 2 minutes, remove from heat, cover and let stand 1 hour. Without draining, bring to a boil again, then reduce heat, cover and simmer until beans are tender (mash several to test), about 45 minutes. Add more water if necessary.

While beans are cooking, fry the bacon over medium heat until crisp. Remove with a slotted spoon, drain and set aside. Pour off all but 2 T. of the drippings, add the onion and saute until translucent. Add ground meat and cook until browned. Stir in tomatoes and liquid, breaking them up with a spoon. Add 1 tsp. salt, sugar, mustard and the cooked beans. Boil, uncovered, until most of the liquid is evaporated. Scatter the bacon over the top just before serving.

*Dorothy Hunter*
B-Bar-C Outfitters
P.O. Box 386
Orofino, ID 83544

## VENISON STEW BASQUE STYLE

Serves: 5
Prep Time: 1½ hours

2 bacon strips, diced
1 T. butter
¾ lb. pearl onions
1½ lbs. venison,
   cut into cubes
1 garlic clove, minced

2 T. flour
1½ cups dry red wine
1 tsp. salt
¼ tsp. pepper
¼ cup brandy

In Dutch oven, saute bacon bits in butter. Add onions and cook until brown, stirring often. Remove bacon and onions and set to the side. Put venison pieces in pan and brown, stirring often. Add wine, salt, pepper, bacon and onions to pan. Bring to a boil, reduce heat and simmer 1 hour, or until tender. Stir in brandy and simmer 3 minutes.

## BRAISED VENISON

Serves: 4
Prep Time: 10 hours

dry marinade mix
4-6 cups dry red wine
2½-3 lbs. venison, cut in cubes

1-2 tsp. flour
1-2 tsp. butter

Marinate meat for 3 to 4 hours in mix. Add red wine, cover and let stand an extra 3 hours. Put meat in large pan, strain marinated sauce and pour liquid over meat to a depth of 1½ to 2 inches. Cook 2 to 2½ hours, covered, on low heat. Add water if necessary. After meat is done, add flour and butter mixture to sauce. Stir until dissolved.

*Andrea Wolaver*
Colorado Drop Camps
P.O. Box 38254
Colorado Springs, CO 80937

# CAMP STEW

Serves: 6
Prep Time: 45-60 minutes

1 lb. meat chunks
1 onion
3 carrots
4 stalks celery
1 lg. can stewed tomatoes

1 sm. can tomato sauce
½ head cabbage
1 T. soy sauce
1 cup water
salt and pepper
garlic salt

Mix all ingredients together. Cook slowly over fire until tender.

# SHEPHERD'S PIE

Serves: 6
Prep Time: 45 minutes

1 T. butter
3 cups hot mashed potatoes
3 cups cold cooked meat chunks
2 cups gravy from meat

Generously butter bottom of pot. Spread mashed potatoes over bottom and up sides. Layer cubed meat on top, pour gravy over that, drop a few spoonfuls of mashed potatoes over all the concoction, cover and cook about 30 minutes.

*Pat Jacobson*
Arctic Rivers Guide Service
Box 1313
Kodiak, AK 99615

# CRYSTAL CREEK BUTTERFLY TENDERLOINS

Serves: 4
Prep Time: 20-30 minutes

| | |
|---|---|
| 1½  lbs. game tenderloins<br>      or steaks | flour<br>salt and pepper |
| 2  eggs, beaten<br>    breadcrumbs | bacon grease |

Butterfly each piece of steak with a sharp knife. (To butterfly: slice sideways through meat, leaving about ⅜ inch of side still together; spread open and press flat.) Mix flour and bread-crumbs together and coat meat. Heat skillet with bacon grease. Dip meat in egg and place in pan. (Be sure to dip in egg last.) Fry until golden on each side, turning as often as necessary, until juices do not seep out. Season each side.

Note: Be sure to cut the meat very thin, rather than the usual ½-1-inch thickness that most sportsmen use. This method should never be more than ¼-⅜ inch maximum when ready for frying. This way they fry fast, and the breading stays on, keeping the meat moist.

*Peg Puche*
Crystal Creek Outfitters
Star Route Box 44A
Jackson Hole, WY 83001

# HOMEMADE EGG NOODLES AND VENISON

Serves: 6
Prep Time: 2 hours at home
             1 hour at camp

| | |
|---|---|
| 6 eggs, beaten | 1-2 quarts homecanned |
| 1 tsp. salt | venison or |
| ¼ tsp. baking powder | 2 lbs. small chunked venison |
| 5 cups flour | 1 onion or ¼ cup dry onion |
| | 2 cubes beef bouillon |

Mix eggs, salt, baking powder and flour until mixture is very stiff. Sprinkle flour on and under mixture on a board and roll as thin as possible. Sift flour over rolled mixture and roll up like cinnamon rolls. Slice in very thin pieces and unroll to dry. Place in airtight container and store in cool place or freezer until your camping trip.

At camp: In a large kettle, heat meat, onion and bouillon in 1½ quarts water until boiling. If using fresh meat allow longer stewing time. Add salt and pepper to taste. Add noodles and simmer at least 30 minutes.

*Mary Beth Kibler*
Kibler Outfitter & Guide Service
Box A-6
Sand Springs, MT 59077

# VENISON BUNDLES TO GO

Serves: 6-8
Prep Time: 45 minutes

1-2 **lbs. ground venison**
  4 **lg. eggs**
  2 **8 oz. cans tomato sauce**
  2 **cups small bread cubes**
  2 **tsp. chili powder**
  1 **tsp. ground cumin**
  1 **tsp. salt**
 16 **taco shells**
  8 **slices American cheese**

Mix together venison, eggs, tomato sauce, bread cubes, chili powder, cummin and salt. Divide into 16 portions. Press each lightly into a taco shell, smoothing surface. Place on a broiler pan rack. Bake at 350 degrees for 20 minutes turn over and bake 20 minutes more. A few minutes before done, place ½ slice cheese on meat in each taco shell. Drain on paper towels. Serve warm with guacamole and sour cream, or add lettuce and tomato slice and serve with a dollop of mayonnaise.

*Walter Squier*
Portland, Connecticut

## PEPPER STEAK

Serves: 12
Prep Time: ½ hour

```
    3  lbs. venison steak
    2  lg. onions, sliced
  4-5  green peppers, sliced
    3  T. cornstarch
  1½  cups cold water
    6  T. soy sauce
    3  tsp. sugar
    3  tsp. garlic salt
   ¾  tsp. pepper
       Minute Rice
   ½  cup cooking oil
```

Preheat oil in large frying pan. Add meat and brown. Remove meat to serving dish. Add onions and pepper slices and cook until tender. Dissolve cornstarch in water and soy sauce. Add sugar, garlic salt and pepper. Pour into skillet with vegetables, stirring until sauce is thickened and clear. Add meat back to pan and simmer several minutes longer or until heated through. Serve over hot rice.

Note: The fixings for this recipe can be dehydrated. With fresh venison it makes a very handy back country meal.

*Teri Olsen*
Yellowater Outfitters
Box 836
Grass Range, MT 59032

# Camp Cooking

## TERIYAKI VENISON STEAK

Serves: 6
Prep Time: several hours

**4-6 venison steaks**

**Marinade:**
- ¼ cup soy sauce
- 1 clove garlic, crushed
- 1 tsp. sugar
- ½ tsp. monosodium glutamate
- 1 tsp. ground ginger
- 1 tsp. powdered AuJus

Mix marinade ingredients. Trim all fat from steaks. Marinade several hours. Broil or barbeque steaks to desired doneness.

## VENISON BROILED FILET MIGNON

Serves: 8
Prep Time: 45 minutes

- 2 lbs. venison tenderloin
- 16 bacon strips
  salt and pepper

Cut venison into 1-inch thick slices. Wrap each piece of meat in a strip of bacon, fastening ends together with a toothpick. Broil until done. Salt and pepper to taste.

*Nancy and Roger Dundas*
Dundas Outfitting
Rt. 1 Box 17A
Toston, MT 59463

## BUCKAROO DINNER

Serves: 4-6
Prep Time: 1½ hours

| | |
|---|---|
| bacon strips | American cheese |
| potatoes | rice, uncooked |
| onion | salt and pepper |
| green pepper | 1 can tomato soup |
| uncooked meatballs | ½ can milk |

Place ingredients in greased casserole in layers. Cover with soup and milk, cook slowly 1½ hours.

*Pat Jacobson*
Arctic Rivers Guide Service
Box 1313
Kodiak, AK 99615

## VENISON HUNGARIAN GOULASH

Serves: 4
Prep Time: 1¼ hours

| | |
|---|---|
| ⅓ cup cooking oil | 1 3-oz. can tomato paste |
| 4 medium onions, chopped | white table wine |
| 2 T. paparika | salt and pepper |
| 3 lbs. venison cubes | |

Saute onions in oil in large saucepan until golden. Remove from heat, add venison cubes and stir in tomato paste. Cover with wine just to the top of the meat. Cover pot, simmer on low heat for 1 hour. If sauce gets too thick, add a little water while it is cooking. Serve with boiled potatoes, noodles or rice.

*Vera Schmidt*
The Driftwood
R.R. 1, Box 260A
Patten, ME 04765

# VENISON HAWAIIAN

Serves: 6
Prep Time: 1½ hours

- 3 lbs. venison
- 3 green peppers
- 1 cup water
- 1 tsp. salt
- 1 can pineapple chunks

Hawaiian sauce:
- 4 T. cornstarch
- ½ cup sugar
- 1¼ cup pineapple juice
- ¼ cup vinegar
- 4 T. soy sauce

Cut meat into 1-inch cubes. Brown on all sides. Add water and salt, simmer gently until meat is tender, about 1 hour. Keep adding water as needed. Clean green peppers and cut into 1-inch squares, boil 5 minutes and drain. Add pepper squares and pineapple chunks to browned meat. Make sauce by mixing cornstarch with a little liquid so it doesn't lump, then combine all ingredients and cook until sauce is thick and clear. Pour sauce over meat mixture, simmer 5 minutes. Serve over Chinese noodles or cooked rice.

*Chuck Watson*
Dundas Outfitting
Rt. 1 Box 17A
Toston, MT 59643

## STUFFED BACK STRAPS

Serves: 4
Prep Time: 3½ hours

|  |  |
|---|---|
| game backstraps | ½ cup melted margarine |
| 1½ loaves stale bread | 2 eggs, beaten |
| 1 lg. onion | 1 cup milk |
| salt and pepper | |
| poultry seasoning | |

Dice onion and mix with other ingredients to make stuffing.
Clean back straps from any game and place a layer in the bottom of a greased pan. Put a layer of stuffing on top of meat, then add another layer of back straps and bake, covered, until meat is tender, about 3 hours. It may be necessary to add a little water from time to time.

G.O.A.B.C.

## STEW WITH DUMPLINGS

Serves: 6
Prep Time: 2½ hours

| | |
|---|---|
| 2 lbs. meat | 2 small onions |
| ½ cup flour | 1 cup cubed carrots |
| 1 tsp. salt | 1 cup cubed turnips |
| ¼ tsp. black pepper | 6 potatoes, quartered |

Wash and dry meat, cut into 2-inch cubes. Combine flour, salt and pepper; dredge meat well. Place fat cut from meat into kettle and brown meat. Add vegetables, simmer about 1 hour. About 20 minutes prior to serving, add drop dumplings, cover and cook. Don't remove lid before serving or dumplings will lose some lightness.

## POTATO DUMPLINGS

Serves: 6
Prep Time: 30 minutes

| | |
|---|---|
| 5 potatoes, grated | 1 T. flour |
| 2 cups bread crumbs | ½ tsp. salt |
| ¼ cup milk | dash of pepper |
| 1 small onion, grated | |
| 2 eggs, beaten | |

Combine potato, bread crumbs, milk and onion. Add beaten eggs, flour, salt and pepper and blend well. Shape mixture into walnut sized balls, roll lightly in flour, drop into boiling salted water. Cover tightly and allow to boil for 15 minutes. Remove to a bowl, add sherry to stew (optional), re-heat and pour over dumplings.

*Pat Jacobson*
Artic Rivers Guide Service
Box 1313
Kodiak, AK 99615

# HIDDEN BASIN BARBEQUE BURGERS

Serves: 4
Prep Time: 1 hour

>     2  eggs
>     2  lbs. ground game meat
>     2  T. Worcestershire
>  1½  tsp. salt
>     ½  tsp. seasoned salt or garlic salt
>         pepper
>         breadcrumbs
>         mushrooms, chopped
>         onions, chopped
>         Cheddar or Swiss cheese, cubed

Beat eggs slightly, add ground meat and seasonings. Mix lightly, then add about ¼ cup dry breadcrumbs for texture. Divide in quarters. Pat out ¼ of the meat to a 7 to 8-inch circle on wax paper. Leave 1 inch margin for sealing, and spread ½ side of the circle with filling of mushrooms, onions and cheese (mixed together). Lift wax paper under the unfilled side, folding over filling and meat. Press around the margin to seal in the filling. Brush top side with salad oil to keep burger from sticking to grill. Place in wire broiler basket. Peel off paper, and brush other side with oil. Broil slowly to allow filling to heat through, flavors to mingle and cheese to melt.

*Peg Puche*
Crystal Creek Outfitters
Star Route Box 44A
Jackson Hole, WY 83001

# HOBO PACKS

Serves: varies
Prep Time: 1 hour

   **ground beef, deer or elk**
**Approximately ¼ cup per serving:**
   **tomatoes, diced**
   **onion, chopped**
   **cabbage, chopped**
   **mushrooms, sliced**
   **bell pepper, chopped**
   **Swiss or American cheese**
   **barbecue sauce**

Make patties out of burger. Place in the center of foil square approximately 14-17" long. Salt and pepper meat. Layer vegetables on top. Add grated cheese and barbecue sauce. Seal foil carefully. Cook on medium hot coals for 15-20 minutes. Eat right out of the foil!

*Paula Del Giudice*
Reno, Nevada

# SIX LAKES SHISH KEBAB

Serves: 6
Prep Time: 4 hours

   ½  cup salad oil
   ¼  cup lemon juice
   1  tsp. salt
   1  tsp. marjoram
   ¼  cup snipped parsley
   1  tsp. thyme
   ½  cup chopped onion
   ½  tsp. pepper
   1  clove garlic, minced
   2  lbs. elk steak or tenderloins, cut in strips
      green peppers, quartered
      onion, sliced thick
      small potatoes, precooked
      mushrooms, whole (fresh)
      tomatoes, quartered
      bacon

In deep bowl combine first 9 ingredients for marinade; mix well. Add meat strips or cubes and stir to coat. Refrigerate overnight or let stand at room temperature for 2 to 3 hours, turning occasionally. When ready to cook, roll up strips of steak and wrap in bacon slices. Fill skewers, alternating meat with vegetables. Broil over hot coals, brushing frequently with melted butter or margarine. Turn often.

*Peg Puche*
Crystal Creek Outfitters
Star Route Box 44A
Jackson Hole, WY 83001

# CURRIED CARIBOU "A LA BIERE"

Serves: 4
Prep Time: 30 minutes

| | |
|---|---|
| 4 lg. fillets of caribou | 1 tsp. curry powder |
| 2 T. butter | 1 can beer |
| 1 onion, sliced | salt and pepper |
| 1 green pepper, sliced | ¼ tsp. parsley |
| 1 can mushrooms, drained | ¼ tsp. thyme |

Fry fillets in butter in a large frying pan. Add all vegetables, season with spices and add beer. Let cook until vegetables soften. Serve with rice.

*Lise Vanasse*
Tunulik Hunting Camp
Fort Chimo, New Quebec JOM 1CO

## CARIBOU STEAK

Serves: 2-4
Prep Time: 1½ hours

| | |
|---|---|
| 1  caribou round steak | ½  tsp. salt |
| 1  onion, chopped | ¼  tsp. pepper |
| 3  T. drippings | ½  tsp. sweet basil |
| 1  cup canned tomatoes | flour |
| ½  cup sour cream | |

Mix enough flour for dredging with the salt and pepper.
Dredge steaks, rubbing flour well into both sides of the meat.
Sear the steaks over hot fire in heavy skillet, using beef drippings. When steaks are well browned on both sides, remove
from pan. Saute onions until soft in drippings. Replace the
steak in the skillet with onions, simmer slowly about 50 minutes,
covered. Mix 2 T. flour into the sour cream, add the tomatoes
and basil and stir well. Pour over steaks, cover and continue
simmering about 25 minutes or until done.

## BRAISED CARIBOU

Serves: 6
Prep Time: 2 hours

| | |
|---|---|
| 3-4  lbs. caribou roast | flour |
| salt and pepper | 3  T. butter |
| 1  cup canned milk | pinch of garlic |

Rub flour, garlic, salt and pepper well into meat. Sear in butter. Pour milk into the baking pan, make sure it covers the bottom of the pan. Place the meat in the pan, cover and bake in
moderate oven, about 35 minutes per pound. Turn meat often.
Add more milk if necessary, as there should be enough milk
left in the pan to make gravy.

*Laurentian Ungava Outfitters*
R.R. 7
Lachute, Quebec J8H 3W9

================= Camp Cooking =================

## CARIBOU STEW WITH DUMPLINGS

Serves: 5-6
Prep Time: 2 hours

| | |
|---|---|
| 2 lbs. caribou meat | 2 potatoes, quartered |
| ½ onion, chopped | salt and pepper |
| ¼ turnip, chopped | ¼ cup flour |
| ¼ cup carrots, chopped | water to cover |
| 2 T. drippings | |

Cut the meat into pieces and dredge with flour, salt and pepper. Brown with onions in oil. Cover with water. Simmer about 2 hours or until tender. Add the vegetables. When done, thicken the gravy with 1 T. flour mixed with a little cold water. Season with salt and pepper. One-half cup strained tomatoes may be added. Serve with dumplings.

## DUMPLINGS

| | |
|---|---|
| 1½ cups flour | ½ cup water or milk |
| 1 tsp. salt | 1 egg |

Beat egg well, add salt and water and stir with flour until a smooth batter is formed. Drop by spoonfuls into the stew. Cover and do not remove cover until dumplings are done.

*Laurentian Ungava Outfitters*
R.R. 7
Lachute, Quebec J8H 3W9

# FOIL LUNCH FOR THE FIRE

Serves: 2
Prep Time: 1 hour

| | |
|---|---|
| 1 lb. ground caribou | 1 lg. onion |
| 10 slices bacon | 1 tsp. salt |
| 3 carrots | 1 tsp. pepper |
| 3 potatoes | 1 tsp. garlic powder |

Spread 5 strips of bacon on foil, (dull side out). Put half the carrots, onions, and potatoes on top. Add spices to the meat and put on top. Add the rest of the vegetables, the bacon and then wrap. Lie on hot coals for ½ hour on each side.

*Kevin Mattice*
Akuliak Caribou Camp
George River, New Quebec J0M 1N0

# CARIBOU STEW

Serves: 5-6
Prep Time: 2 hours

| | |
|---|---|
| 2 lbs. caribou meat | ½ tsp. pepper |
| 2 T. oil | ¼ tsp. oregano |
| 1 cup onion, thinly sliced | 1 cup dry wine |
| 1 clove garlic, minced | 1 T. tomato paste |
| 1½ tsp. salt | ½ cup boiling water |

Cut meat into stew size pieces. Heat the oil in Dutch oven or heavy pan. Saute the onions and garlic until soft. Add the meat and brown. Season with salt, pepper, oregano and add the wine, tomato paste and water. Bring to a boil, cover and cook at a low simmer 1½ hours or until done. If potatoes, carrots or turnips are desired, add to the stew 45 minutes before stew is done, adding more water to cook.

*Jack Hume Adventures Inc.*
R.R. 7
Lachute, Quebec J8H 3W9

# MOOSE STROGANOFF

Serves: 6
Prep Time: 45 minutes

1½ lbs. moose meat
¼ cup flour
1 tsp. salt
2 small onions, diced
½ lb. mushrooms
1 clove garlic, minced
3 T. oil
2 T. flour
1 cup beef bouillon
1 T. Worcestershire
1 cup sour cream
   steamed rice

Cut moose into ½-inch strips, roll in ¼ cup flour and salt. Saute onions, mushrooms, and garlic in oil for 5 minutes. Add meat, brown evenly. Remove meat, mushrooms, onion from pan. Combine 2 T. flour with drippings in pan. Add bouillon and Worcestershire. Cook until thickened. Add sour cream; heat slowly until gravy simmers. Add meat and vegetables, heat briefly. Serve over rice if desired.

*Pat Jacobson*
Arctic Rivers Guide Service
Box 1313
Kodiak, AK 99615

# LOUIE'S MEADOW MOOSE LOAF

Serves: 6-8
Prep Time: 4 hours

| | |
|---|---|
| 3 lbs. ground moose | 1 tsp. Worcestershire |
| 1 celery heart | ½ tsp. chili powder |
| 1 cup grated cheddar cheese | ½ tsp. pepper |
| 2 T. chopped pimento | ⅛ tsp. liquid smoke |
| ½ cup quick rolled oats | 2 eggs, beaten |
| ½ cup evaporated milk | ½ cup chopped green onion |
| 1 T. seasoned salt | ¼ cup chopped green pepper |
| 1 tsp. garlic powder | 1 lb. sliced bacon |

Cut celery heart to about 8 to 9 inches long, wash and dry. Keep bottom of celery heart intact; do not remove root. Gently pull branches apart and sprinkle with salt. Combine cheese and pimento and spread between celery branches. Wrap heart tightly in foil, pressing branches firmly together. Chill while preparing loaf.

Combine remaining ingredients except bacon. Turn meat onto large sheet of waxed paper and pat out to an oval, approximately 11x12 inches. Cut off only the very bottom of root of celery heart and place on center of meat. Fold meat up over celery, rolling to surround the heart. Pat into a loaf. Lay bacon slices in pattern over top of meat, slightly overlapping slices. Gently lift loaf on one side and tuck bacon ends under. Repeat other side. Use wooden picks to hold bacon ends in place if needed. Tie loaf securely with string. Wrap in foil, sealing top, but do not close ends. Insert spit through center of celery and balance. Close ends of foil around spit. Using a line of hot coals on each side of loaf and a drip pan underneath, let meat rotate for 1¼ hours. Remove foil carefully and cook 20 minutes more. Slice crosswise to serve.

*Peg Puche*
Crystal Creek Outfitters
Star Route Box 44A
Jackson Hole, WY 83001

================ **Camp Cooking** ================

# MOOSE BURGUNDY

Serves: 4
Prep Time: 2½ hours

| | |
|---|---|
| 2 lbs. moose | ⅛ tsp. pepper |
| 1 can mushroom soup | 12 small whole white onions |
| ¼ cup burgundy wine | 2 cups sliced mushrooms |
| 2 T. chopped parsley | |

Cut moose into 1¼-inch cubes and brown in oil. Pour off oil and add soup, wine, parsley and pepper. Cover; cook over low heat for 1½ hours. Add onions and mushrooms, cover and cook 1 hour more. Serve over wide noodles.

*Vera Schmidt*
The Driftwood
R.R. 1, Box 260A
Patten, ME 04765

========== Camp Cooking ==========

## MOOSE DINNER IN FOIL

Serves: 6
Prep Time: 1½ hours

| | |
|---|---|
| 1½ lbs. moose | 2 T. water |
| 1 pkg. mushroom soup mix | ½ lb. mushrooms |
| 1 pkg. onion soup mix | ¼ cup white wine |
| 3 carrots, quartered | salt and pepper |
| 3 stalks celery, cut | garlic powder |
| 3 potatoes, quartered | |

Cut meat into 1-inch pieces and spread on foil. Combine soup mixes and a dab of water to make thick consistency. Spread over meat. Top with vegetables. Sprinkle water over veggies. Fold foil and crimp edges. Cook about 1½ hours or until tender.

*Pat Jacobson*
Arctic Rivers Guide Service
Box 1313
Kodiak, Alaska 99615

## BIRTHDAY CREEK MOOSE NOSE

Serves: 2-3
Prep Time: 24 hours

| | |
|---|---|
| 1 fresh moose nose | salt and pepper |
| 1 small onion, sliced thinly | paprika |
| 2 cloves garlic | |

First bag yourself a moose, preferably an Alaskan moose (they have the biggest noses). Clean the nose by skinning and removing all hair. Cut the meat into small cubes and cover with water. Add the garlic, onion, salt and pepper. Let boil until tender. Remove from fire or stove and let chill. Serve cold in the jellied broth.

*"Alaska" Rick Sinchak*
Warren, Ohio

# YOU WON'T BELIEVE IT'S COUGAR!

Serves: 2-3
Prep Time: 1¼ hours

| | |
|---|---|
| ¼ cup soy sauce | 1 lb. sliced bacon |
| 2-4 lbs. cougar meat | 6 oz. beer |
| 1½ T. minced garlic | ¼ tsp. liquid smoke |
| 2 T. Worcestershire | ¼ tsp. pepper |

Mix all ingredients except bacon and meat in a bowl. Trim all fat and gristle from meat and then cut into small pieces. Soak meat in mixture for ½ hour. Wrap ½ the meat in bacon strips, secure them with a toothpick and then fry until done. Fry the remaining meat without bacon for a different taste. You can flour or bread the meat prior to cooking if desired.

*Jeff Gleave*
JG Guides & Outfitters
P.O. Box 41
Monroe, UT 84754

If you litter with disgrace,
    and spoil the beauty of this place,
May indigestion rack your chest,
    and ants invade your pants and vest.

## BREADED LION LOIN

Serves: 8
Prep Time: 2 hours

   2 **lion backstraps**
   4 **eggs**
   2 **cups flour**
   1 **tsp. garlic salt**
   1 **tsp. salt**
   1 **tsp. pepper**
     **cooking oil**

Cut meat into ½-inch slices. Whip eggs until smooth. Dip meat in eggs, then in flour. Fry in medium-hot skillet until batter is crisp on both sides. If meat is tough, pound with knife first.

*Bryce Pinning*
Dry Creek Hunts
Rt. 3
Delta, UT 84624

# BUFFALO HUMP ROAST

Take one 45-70 single shot rifle or if not available, bow and arrow o.k.

Find and stalk one fat buffalo.

Dress out carefully.

Take 4-pound roast from the hump and roast over an open fire for five hours.

Take 10 ounces Canadian Club and mix with clear creek water.

Drink slowly while roast is cooking.

When done to perfection (the roast), slice and eat with fresh bannock.

Serves one hunter. For more people, cook more hump and use more "C.C."

## SAUSAGE AND PEPPERS

Serves: varies
Prep Time: ½ hour

**2 large Italian or kielbasa sausages, cut into 3-inch pieces, per serving**
**½ bell pepper, sliced, per serving**
**¼ onion, chopped, per serving**
**French rolls, if desired**

Heat oil in large skillet or Dutch oven. Add sausage and fry until cooked through. Pour off extra oil. Add pepper and onions. Fry lightly.

Serve over French rolls, if desired.

*Paula Del Giudice*
Reno, Nevada

## BEER BRAISED RABBIT

Serves: 4
Prep Time: 1 hour

**2  lbs. rabbit**
   **salt and pepper**
**3  T. oil**
**3  potatoes, halved**
**3  carrots, cut**
**1  onion, sliced**
**1  cup beer**
**¼  cup chili sauce**
**1  T. brown sugar**
**1  clove garlic, minced**
**⅓  cup cold water**
**3  T. flour**
**½  tsp. salt**

Cut rabbit into pieces and season generously with salt and pepper. In Dutch oven, brown rabbit in oil. Add potatoes, carrots and onions. In a bowl, combine the beer, chili sauce, brown sugar and garlic. Pour over rabbit. Cover and simmer 1 hour or until tender. Remove meat and vegetables to a warm serving platter. Measure pan juices. Add more beer or water if necessary to make 1½ cups. Return juices to Dutch oven. Combine water, flour and salt, stir into pan juices. Cook and stir until thickened and bubbly. Return meat and vegetables to gravy; heat through.

*W.D. Helper Jr.*
Monroe, Utah

## COOKOUT RABBIT

Serves: 6
Prep Time: 1½ hours

  2-3  **lbs. rabbit, cut in serving pieces**
  1½  **tsp. salt**
   ¼  **tsp. pepper**
   ½  **cup sherry**
   ½  **cup cooking oil**
  1½  **tsp. seasoned salt**

Season moist pieces of rabbit with salt and pepper. Place pan of rabbit over medium-hot bed of coals. Make sauce by mixing remaining ingredients. Keep rabbit well basted with this sauce, turning pieces frequently. Cook 1 hour or until tender. Your own favorite barbeque sauce may be used but some added oil will help keep rabbit juicy.

*Pat Jacobson*
Arctic Rivers Guide Service
Box 1313
Kodiak, AK 99615

# BLUE GROUSE WITH WILD RICE

Serves: 4
Prep Time: 1 hour

   1  **blue grouse**
   1  **cup flour**
      **parsley**
   ½  **cup butter**
   ½  **pint whipping cream**
   1  **cup mushrooms**
   ½  **cup chopped onions**
   1  **cup cooking wine**
      **wild rice**

Combine flour, salt and pepper. Roll grouse in mixture and brown in butter. Remove grouse. Add mushrooms and onions and cook until done. Return grouse to pan, add wine and simmer 30 minutes. Remove grouse, add whipping cream to drippings. Stir until smooth. Arrange over wild rice on warm platter.

*Jeff Wolaver*
Colorado Drop Camps
P.O. Box 38254
Colorado Springs, CO 80937

A  is for Ann, whose roast caught fire,

B  is for Betty, whose stove did tire.

C  is for Connie, who made homemade brew,

D  is for Debby, who put peppers in the stew.

E  is for Ester, who tried wild mushrooms,

F  is for Frances, who couldn't stand fumes.

G  is for Gwen, who dieted too long,

H  is for Helen, whose oven went wrong.

I  is for Iva, whose husband could cook,

J  is for Joan, who went by the book.

K  is for Kaye, who saw her grocery bill,

L  is for Lynn, who ate her fill.

M  is for Maxine, who believes in women's lib,

N  is for Nancy, who swallowed a rib.

O  is for Olive, who took to drinking,

P  is for Pat, whose dumplings kept sinking.

Q  is for Queeny, who couldn't boil water,

R  is for Rose, who was no smarter.

S  is for Sandra, whose supper burned,

T  is for Toots, who never learned,

U  is for Una, who fell off a chair,

V  is for Vi, who didn't care.

W  is for Winnie, who ran out of flour,

X  is for Xena, who cooked every hour.

Y  is for Yvonne, who overdid a feast.

Z  is for Zetta, who did not . . . . . . .
                    Rest in Peace.

# DUCK BREAST FRY

Serves: 2
Prep Time: 45 minutes

**2 duck breasts, skinned**
**2 eggs, slightly beaten**
**5 T. whole wheat flour**
**5 T. butter**
**1 tsp. curry**

Mix curry and flour together. Melt 2 T. butter in frying pan. Slice breasts in half through the middle. Dip each piece in the eggs, then in flour and repeat. Place breasts in hot butter. Turn to brown both sides and cook, uncovered, for 25 minutes, adding remaining butter as needed.

*Saskatchewan River Hunting Camp*
129 First St. E.
Saskatoon, Saskatchewan 57H 1R6

## EASY COCONUT DESSERT

Serves: varies
Prep Time: 5 minutes

> **milk**
> **eggs**
> **coconut**
> **sugar, to taste**
> **slices of bread, cut into strips 1-inch wide**

Whisk eggs into milk. Add coconut and sugar. Dip strips of
bread into mixture. Don't allow bread to become too soaked.
Cook over coals on a grill until lightly browned. Or skewer the
bread on sticks and let the kids cook their own over the coals.

*Paula Del Giudice*
Reno, Nevada

## APPLE MARSHMALLOW SANDWICHES

Serves: 1
Prep Time: 5 minutes

> 1 **apple**
> 2 **T. peanut butter**
> 1 **lg. marshmallow**

Remove core from apple and slice into pieces approximately
¼-inch thick. Toast marshmallow over fire. Spread peanut butter on one side of apple, put marshmallow on top of peanut butter. Put another slice of apple on top and squeeze together to
make a sandwich.

*Stephen Thompson*
East Berne, New York

# CHOCOLATE CRAZY CAKE

Serves: 6-8
Prep Time: 45 minutes

    3 cups flour
    2 cups sugar
    ⅓ cup cocoa
    1 tsp. salt
    2 tsp. soda
    2 T. vinegar
    2 tsp. vanilla
    ¾ cup oil
    2 cups cold water

Mix dry ingredients (can be mixed ahead and put in recloseable plastic bags). Add the liquid ingredients and stir. Do not beat. Pour into ungreased 9x13 pan. Bake at 350 degrees for 35 to 40 minutes.

Note: To use in Dutch oven, use only ½ of the dry ingredients for each batch. Reduce the liquid ingredients accordingly.

*Nancy Dundas*
Dundas Outfitting
Route 1 Box 17A
Toston, MT 59643

- For an easy dessert, dissolve coffee-mate in skim milk and whip to use on boiled rice and raisins.

- Four cups fresh berries takes ¾ to 1 cup sugar for pie or pudding.

- When sprinkling sugar on cookies, put it into a salt shaker. It saves time.

- To moisten brown sugar which has already hardened, place apple slices in container with sugar and cover tightly.

- For variety in instant pudding, top with browned coconut, whipped cream or canned peaches.

- For a delicious easy dessert, cover plain cake with instant pudding and top with whipped cream.

- To make sour milk, add 1 T. vinegar, lemon or pickle juice to 1 cup milk.

- To soften white sugar lumps, place in a brown paper bag and heat in 300 degree oven for approximately 10 minutes or until granules are separated.

- A mashed banana added to the white of an egg and beaten stiff makes a delicious substitute for whipped cream.

- When whipping cream is required, add the white of an egg to the cream before whipping. It will whip in half the time, the cream will be stiffer and it will not affect the flavor.

- Put jello in a tin pot with a tight fitting lid and place in a shallow stream so that the water comes to within one inch of the top. Jello will set in about 1½ hours. Be careful if the stream has a tendency to rise or the jello will be a little watery.

# SPICED BLUEBERRIES

Yield: 6
Prep Time: 1 ¼ hours

| | |
|---|---|
| 8 cups blueberries | ½ tsp. cloves |
| ½ cup vinegar | 2 cups sugar |
| 1 tsp. cinnamon | |

Wash and clean berries. Put berries, vinegar and spices into a pan and bring to a boil. Cook for 20 minutes. Add sugar and cook another 40 minutes or until thick. Stir frequently. Do not scorch mixture. Pour mixture into sterile jars and seal, or eat immediately.

# BLUEBERRY COBBLER

Yield: 6
Prep Time: 25 minutes

| | |
|---|---|
| 1 cup water | 1 tsp. baking powder |
| ½ cup sugar | 2 T. sugar |
| 1 tsp. lemon juice | ¼ tsp. salt |
| ⅛ tsp. allspice | 1 egg, well beaten |
| 3 cups blueberries | ½ cup milk |
| 1 cup flour | |

Put water, sugar, lemon juice and allspice in a pan and bring to a boil. Add blueberries and simmer for 3 minutes. Put lid on pan. Sift flour, baking powder, sugar and salt together. Combine egg and milk and add to dry ingredients. Stir to make soft dough. Drop dough by teaspoonfuls into simmering berries. Cover and cook for 10 to 12 minutes. Serve hot with cream or sauce.

*Pat Jacobson*
Arctic Rivers Guide Service
Box 1313
Kodiak, AK 99615

## ICELANDIC FRUIT CAKE

Serves: several
Prep Time: ½ hour

graham wafers
½ lb. dates

1 T. brown sugar
½ cup water

Boil dates, brown sugar and water together until dates are soft. The mixture should be of jam consistency. Cool. Place a layer of graham wafers on something with a flat surface, then add a layer of date mixture, then a layer of graham wafers and so forth, ending up with a layer of wafers. Spread top and sides with chocolate icing. This is a quick delicious cake and requires no baking.

G.O.A.B.C.

## BLUEBERRY PIE

Serves: 6
Prep Time: 1½ hours

3 cups blueberries
1 cup sugar
¼ cup flour
pinch of salt

1 T. lemon juice
2 T. butter
2 pie crusts

Combine blueberries, sugar, flour, salt and lemon juice. Pour mixture into crust and add a dab of butter. Put on top crust and cut vents. Bake at 450 degrees for 10 minutes, then reduce heat to 350 degrees and bake for another 40 minutes.

*Pat Jacobson*
Arctic Rivers Guide Service
Box 1313
Kodiak, AK 99615

# LLOYD'S CARROT PUDDING

Serves: several
Prep Time: 3½ hours

| | |
|---|---|
| 1 **cup raw potato** | ½ **cup raisins** |
| 1 **cup raw carrots** | 1 **cup cherries** |
| 2 **eggs** | ½ **tsp. cloves** |
| ½ **cup butter** | ½ **tsp. nutmeg** |
| 1 **cup brown sugar** | 1 **tsp. baking soda** |
| ½ **tsp. cinnamon** | 1½ **cups flour** |

Grate 1 cup raw potato and 1 cup raw carrots. Mix together
with eggs, butter, brown sugar, raisins, cherries and spices and
add to the grated carrots. Add 1 teaspoon baking soda to the
potatoes and add to carrot mixture. Add 1½ cups flour. Use a
container with a tight lid (tobacco tins, peanut butter cans or
jars) and fill half full. Steam for 3 hours in a covered kettle.
May be served hot with a sauce or sliced cold.

# CARAMEL SAUCE FOR CARROT PUDDING

Prep Time: 10 minutes

| | |
|---|---|
| ½ **cup butter or margarine** | ⅛ **tsp. salt** |
| 1 **cup brown sugar** | 2 **cups boiling water** |
| 2 **T. flour** | 1 **tsp. vanilla** |

Melt margarine; add sugar, flour and salt. Let bubble but not
boil. Remove from heat and add boiling water, stirring constantly. Add vanilla. This is meant to be a very thin sauce for
the heavy pudding.

G.O.A.B.C.

# BOILED CAKE

Serves: several
Prep Time: 1 hour

          3  cups hot water
          3  tsp. cinnamon
     1½  cup lard or butter
        ½  tsp. cloves
          3  cups sugar
          1  tsp. nutmeg
          3  cups raisins
          3  tsp. baking soda
              flour

Put all ingredients, except soda and flour, into a large
saucepan and boil for 1 minute. Take from heat and add 3
heaping teaspoons soda, while still boiling. Stir until all foam
has settled. Let cool. Add enough flour to make a thick batter
(approximately 6 cups). Be sure to put in a large pan or it will
run over when the soda is added. Bake at 350 degrees.

G.O.A.B.C.

# PHEASANT CORN CHOWDER

Serves: 6-8
Prep Time: several hours

  2  pheasants
  1  cup celery, chopped
  1  chicken bouillon cube
  1  potato, cubed
  1  pkg. frozen corn
  ½  cup mushrooms, chopped
  2  cups milk
  3  drops Tabasco sauce
  4  T. butter
  1  tsp. pimento, chopped
     paprika
     salt and pepper
     parsley

Stew pheasant in one quart water with celery, bouillon and onion until the legs are tender. Cool and strip meat carefully from the bones. Chop into bite-size pieces. Use broth as the base for chowder. Add enough water to make one quart liquid. Add potatoes and cook for 15 minutes. Add corn, cook 5 minutes. Add meat, mushrooms, stir in milk slowly, add Tabasco, butter, pimento, paprika, salt and pepper. Serve garnished with parsley.

*E. Jenkins*
Elkland, Pennsylvania

# PHEASANT CACCIATORE

Serves: 6-8
Prep Time: 4 hours

8-10 pheasant breasts
  2 cups Italian bread crumbs
  ¼ cup Parmesan cheese
  ¼ cup Romano cheese
  3 eggs
  ½ cup milk or water
  1 15 oz. can tomato paste
  1 lg. can stewed tomatoes
  1 lg. onion, chopped
  1 can mushrooms, drained

1 green pepper, cut
1 cup red wine
2-3 cloves garlic, minced
2 T. dried sweet basil
1 T. oregano
½ T. parsley
1 T. sugar
½ cup Parmesan cheese
  salt and pepper

Mix together the bread crumbs, ¼ cup each Parmesan and
Romano cheese. In another bowl, mix 3 eggs and ½ cup milk.
Dredge breasts in crumbs, then eggs and then crumbs again.
Brown in olive oil in a large frying pan over medium heat.
Drain on paper towels. In a large pot mix the remaining ingredients. Place breasts in sauce and simmer gently at least 2 to 3
hours. Serve over any type of pasta that you like and top it off
with a generous pile of grated mozzarella cheese. (Skinned,
boned and pounded quail or chicken breasts may be used instead of pheasant.)

*Pamela Messina*
Glenview, Illinois

# PHEASANT OR QUAIL CORDON BLEU

Serves: 8
Prep Time: 1½ hours

        2  lbs. pheasant breast or
       24  quail breasts
        ½  cup Canadian bacon, diced
       1½  cup grated Gruyer or Swiss cheese
        1  small clove garlic, minced
           pepper
        ¼  tsp. thyme leaves
        ½  cup and 3 T. dry white wine
        1  tsp. salt
        ½  cup flour
        3  eggs
        ¼  cup and 1 T. olive oil
       1½  cup fine bread crumbs
        6  T. butter

Cut whole breats in half. In small bowl combine cheese, garlic,
pepper, 3 T. wine, thyme, ½ tsp. salt and Canadian bacon.
Make a pocket in each breast and stuff with mixture.
Refrigerate, covered, for 1 hour. On wax paper, combine flour,
salt and pepper. Beat eggs and 1 T. oil. Coat each breast in
flour mixture, then dip in egg mixture, then in bread crumbs,
coating well. In a large skillet, heat butter and brown breasts
on each side. Turn heat down to low and continue to cook, uncovered, for 20 to 25 minutes.

*Theodore Vasilik*
Freehold, New Jersey

# FOOLPROOF DUCK IN ORANGE SAUCE

Serves: 2-4
Prep Time: 2 hours

- 1 **wild duck**
- 1 **pkg. brown gravy mix**
- ¼ **cup flour**
- 1 **tsp. salt**
- 2 **T. sugar**
- 2 **T. orange marmalade**
- 1 **6 oz. can frozen orange juice, thawed**
- 1 **oven cooking bag**
- 1 **cup hot water**

Wash duck and wipe dry, inside and out. Combine next 6 ingredients and mix well. Add to hot water in the cooking bag and mix well. Place duck in bag and close according to directions. Place in roasting pan and cut slits in top of bag. Bake at 350 degrees for 2 hours. Serve with pan gravy. More than one duck may be cooked in each bag.

*Bobby Wright*
Highland, Indiana

# ORANGE GLAZED SAUCE

Yield: 4½ cups
Prep Time: 5 minutes

- 18 **oz. barbeque sauce**
- 18 **oz. orange marmalade jam**

Blend the bottle of barbeque sauce with the jar of orange marmalade. Use this to baste meat the last 30 minutes of cooking.

*John Zanon*
Norway, Michigan

# CURRANT DUCKS

Serves: 2-4
Prep Time: 1½ hours

2 ducks
1 cup bread crumbs
cooking oil
1 tsp. salt
1 tsp. pepper
2 bay leaves
2 whole cloves
¼ tsp. garlic salt
⅓ cup vinegar
½ cup catsup
2 T. Worcestershire
1 T. A-1 sauce
1 tsp. Kitchen Bouquet
½ cup red currant jelly

Fillet breasts. Dip breasts and legs in beaten eggs and roll in bread crumbs. Brown in oil. Mix all ingredients except jelly with ½ cup water. Pour over meat and bake at 325 degrees for one hour. Add jelly, mixing with water to make a thick sauce. Simmer 10 minutes. If necessary, add water during cooking to maintain liquid state of the sauce.

*Ross Hadfield*
Meridian, Idaho

## TEAL IN WINE SAUCE

Serves: 4
Prep Time: 1½-2 hours

| | |
|---|---|
| 4 small ducks or duck breasts | 1 bay leaf |
| 4 T. butter | 2 cloves |
| 2 T. flour | ½ tsp. Tabasco |
| 1 cup red wine | salt and pepper |
| 2 cups beef broth | ½ tsp. parsley |
| 2 onions, sliced thin | |

Brown ducks in butter until golden brown. Transfer to deep pot or casserole. Add flour to butter and thicken. Stir in the other ingredients except parsley. Bring to a boil, then simmer for 5 minutes, stirring often. Pour sauce over ducks and add parsley. Simmer 1½ hours.

*Bobby Wright*
Highland, Indiana

## WINE SAUCE

Yield: 2 cups
Prep Time: 15 minutes

| | |
|---|---|
| 2 T. butter | ¼ cup heavy cream |
| 2 T. flour | 1 T. white wine |
| 1½ cup chicken broth | dash of white pepper |

In small saucepan, melt the butter. Mix in flour until smooth, add chicken broth all at once. Cook, stirring until smooth and bubbly. Stir in cream, wine and pepper, seasoning to taste. Heat and serve.

*Theodore Vasilik*
Freehold, New Jersey

## CURRIED QUAIL

Serves: 2
Prep Time: 1 hour

| | |
|---|---|
| 4 quail, each cut in half | 1 can cream of mushroom soup |
| 1 medium onion or | 4 T. curry powder |
| 8 large shallots | parsley |
| salt and pepper to taste | long grain and wild rice |

Rub each quail half with salt and pepper and place in roasting pan. Slice the onions on top. Sprinkle on curry powder and parsley and pour the soup over. Roast at 350 degrees for 50 minutes. Serve with rice mixture.

*Theodore Vasilik*
Ft. Myers, Florida

## PTARMIGAN PIE

Serves: 2-3
Prep Time: 1½ hours

| | |
|---|---|
| a couple of ptarmigan | onion powder |
| biscuit dough | garlic powder |
| milk or cream | parsley flakes |
| butter | basil |

Split the dressed ptarmigan down the back. Make a biscuit dough with milk or cream for the mixing. Roll thinly and spread with butter. Fold again and roll. Line a large baking pan with the dough. Lay the ptarmigan in the pan, sprinkle with salt and pepper. Spread each bird with butter and sprinkle onion and garlic powders on them. Boil 2½ cups water with basil and parsley flakes. Add the boiling water and cover with crust. Make small slits to release the steam and bake in a medium oven until done.

*"Alaska" Rick Sinchak*
*Warren, Ohio*

## WILD TURKEY TIDBITS

Serves: 3-4
Prep Time: 45 minutes

- **2 lbs. wild turkey**
- **½ cup corn oil**
- **cracker crumbs or meal**
- **3 eggs**
- **salt and pepper**

Cut turkey into bite-size pieces. Beat eggs in large bowl and set aside. Dip turkey bits in egg, then roll in crumbs. Fry on medium heat in oil until golden brown. Salt and pepper to taste.

*Ramon Acosta*
Mathias, West Virginia

## WILD GROUSE DELUXE

Serves 4-6:
Prep Time: 1-1½ hours

- 3 grouse
- 1 tsp. salt
- 1 tsp. pepper
  garlic salt
- 1 can golden mushroom soup
- 1 egg, slightly beaten
- ½ cup milk
- 1 cup flour
- ¼ cup butter
- ½ cup oil
- 1 cup water

Clean grouse and cut into serving pieces. Dip pieces in mixture of egg, milk, salt, pepper, garlic salt, and roll in flour. Put butter and oil in skillet and heat. Brown grouse on all sides. Remove from skillet and place in a single layer in pan. Add drippings from skillet to mushroom soup and mix well. Spoon over pieces of grouse. Add water to bottom of pan. Cover with foil and bake at 350 degrees for 1 hour until tender.

*Sweet Sue*
Narraway River Outfitting
Box 177
Goodfare, Alberta T0H 1T0

## FOILED GAME BIRDS

Serves: 6
Prep Time: 1 hour

    **2 lbs. meat**
       **whole wheat flour**
       **salt and pepper**
    **2 T. butter**
       **table wine**

Shake birds in flour, salt and pepper. Heat butter in heavy skillet, brown on all sides. Place in foil with a dab of wine, fold and crimp (make several packages). Bake about 30 minutes.

*Pat Jacobson*
Arctic Rivers Guide Service
Box 1313
Kodiak, AK 99615

## SMOTHERED BIRD

Serves: 2-4
Prep Time: 50 minutes

    **3 upland birds**
    **8 juniper berries, crushed**
    **3 T. butter**

Skin birds and remove legs. Mix berries into butter and place inside each bird, keeping a small amount to rub over the outside. Wrap birds in foil, breast side down, and bake at 350 degrees for 40 minutes.

*Glen Hill*
Saskatchewan River Hunting Camps
129 First St. E.
Saskatoon, Saskatchewan S7H 1R6

## HARE STEW

Serves: 6-8
Prep Time: 30 minutes

1 rabbit
8 lg. potatoes, cubed
6 stalks celery, sliced
6 carrots, sliced
1 can peas
1 can corn
1 cup cabbage, shredded

2 bay leaves
1 T. seasoned salt
2 cloves garlic, crushed
2 tsp. poultry seasoning
   pepper
4 chicken bouillon cubes

Boil rabbit until tender enough to pick meat from bones. Peel
vegetables and cut. Pick meat from rabbit, put back in broth
and add all other ingredients. Cover and cook on low heat for 4
to 5 hours. Cover with dumplings.

*Haven Post*
Sturgis, Michigan

## SAUTE RABBIT LA PAN

Serves: 6-8
Prep Time: 6 hours

2 rabbits
¾ cup olive oil
3 cups onion, chopped
1 cup peppers, chopped
1 cup celery, chopped
2 cloves garlic, chopped

1 T. parsley flakes
2 T. Worcestershire
½ tsp. hot sauce
2 tsp. salt
2 cups white wine

Cut rabbit into serving pieces and salt and pepper. Place oil in
a Dutch oven and heat. Brown the rabbit. Add all ingredients
and mix well. Turn heat to low and simmer, covered, about 6
hours or until larger pieces of meat start to fall apart. Serve
over rice.

*Bobby Wright*
Highland, Indiana

# RABBIT AND SQUIRREL MEAT LOAF

Serves: 4-5
Prep Time: 1¾ hours

| | | | |
|---|---|---|---|
| 2 | rabbits | ½ | tsp. pepper |
| 2 | squirrels | 1 | onion, diced |
| 1½ | cups bread crumbs | ¾ | cup celery, diced |
| 2 | eggs | 1 | chicken bouillon cube |
| 1 | tsp. sage | ½ | cup hot water |
| 1 | tsp. salt | | |

Bone rabbit and squirrel while raw. Grind meat, add remaining ingredients and mix well. Shape into loaf. Bake at 350 degrees for 1 hour, covered. Water may be added to prevent drying.

*Robert Lent*
Limestone, New York

# SQUIRREL STEW WITH DUMPLINGS

Serves: 6
Prep Time: 4½ hours

3-5 squirrels, quartered
2 tsp. salt
½ tsp. paprika
    pepper
4 T. butter
2 cups water
2 onions, chopped

1 tsp. poultry seasoning
1 pkg. dry onion soup mix
1 can cream of chicken soup
1 can cream of mushroom soup
2 soup cans water
5 medium potatoes, cubed
3 stalks celery, sliced
6 medium carrots, sliced

Melt butter in a Dutch oven. Add squirrel and cook until browned on all sides. Add water, onions, poultry seasoning and onion soup mix. Mix well, cover and simmer for 30 minutes. Add chicken soup, mushroom soup, water, potatoes, celery and carrots. Cover and cook until done, about 3 hours.

## DUMPLINGS

3 cups buttermilk baking mix
1 cup milk

Mix well and drop by spoonfuls into stew. Cover and simmer 15 minutes. Uncover and cook 10 minutes more.

*Brenda Silagi*
Carmichael, California

# SMALL GAME ENCHILADAS

Serves: 12
Prep Time: 30 minutes

  any small game
1 brick Monterey Jack cheese w/jalapeno peppers
¾ cup onion
1 tsp. oregano
1 pkg. corn tortillas

SAUCE:
3 inches from brick of Velveeta cheese
⅓ cup hot salsa
1 16 oz. can whole tomatoes
1 lb. sour cream
1 can cream of mushroom soup

Boil meat, cool and shred into mixing bowl. Add Monterey Jack cheese, onion and oregano. Melt Velveeta in double boiler. While cheese is melting, put tomatoes, sour cream, mushroom soup and salsa into a blender and mix thoroughly. Add to melted cheese and keep warm.

Roll meat mixture in tortilla shells. Line up shells in pan. Pour sauce over. Bake at 350 degrees for 35 minutes or until lightly brown.

*Haven Post*
Sturgis, Michigan

## VENISON MEATBALLS

Serves: 6-8
Prep Time: 3-4 hours

2 lbs. ground venison
1 lb. hot Italian sausage
2 cups fresh bread crumbs
1 onion, minced
2 lg. cloves garlic, minced
2 eggs
1 tsp. dried sweet basil

½ tsp. dried oregano
½ tsp. parsley
¼ cup Romano cheese
¼ cup Parmesan cheese
1 tsp. fennel seed
1 tsp. Italian seasoning
salt and pepper

Combine all ingredients in a large bowl and thoroughly mix together with hands. Shape into balls and slowly brown in a large frying pan. Add to spaghetti sauce, simmer for at least 3 hours uncovered. Stir often. Serve on any kind of pasta.

*Pamela Messina*
Glenview, Illinois

## VENISON SPAGHETTI

Serves: 6-8
Prep Time: 1-1½ hours

2 lbs. ground venison
2 lg. onions, chopped
½ green pepper, chopped
2 cloves garlic, chopped
2 stalks celery, chopped

olive oil
salt and pepper
32 oz. spaghetti sauce

Brown onion, green pepper, garlic and celery in olive oil. Add ground venison and brown. Add salt and pepper. Add spaghetti sauce. Bring to a boil, then simmer 15 minutes or until juices become thick.

*Sue Volkmann*
Pittsburgh, New Hampshire

# SICILIAN SPAGHETTI SAUCE WITH VENISON

Serves: 6-8
Prep Time: 3-4 hours

**MEAT:**
- 2 lbs. ground venison
- 1 lb. hot Italian sausage
- 1 lg. onion, chopped
- 1 rib celery, chopped
- 3 cloves garlic, minced
- 1 tsp. fennel seed
- ⅓ cup olive oil
- ⅓ cup Romano cheese
- salt and pepper

**SAUCE:**
- 2 lg. cans tomato sauce
- 1 6 oz. can tomato paste
- 1 can mushrooms
- 1 green pepper, chopped
- 3½ tsp. dried sweet basil
- 2 tsp. dried oregano
- 1 tsp. dried parsley
- 1 tsp. Italian seasonings
- 2 tsp. sugar
- salt and pepper
- 1 clove garlic, minced
- ¼ cup Parmesan cheese
- 1 lg. tomato, diced
- 1 cup red wine

Cook the onion and celery in olive oil in a 6-quart Dutch oven. Add the Italian sausage (remove from skin if necessary) and venison. Add all other meat ingredients except cheese. Cook until browned. Drain off all grease and return meat to pot. Place over low heat and add Romano cheese. Stir until cheese is melted. Add all sauce ingredients. Simmer over low heat, uncovered, for at least 3 hours. Stir often with a wooden spoon. This is best if refrigerated overnight and served the next day, giving the sauce a chance to blend. Serve sauce over any type of pasta you like.

*Pamela Messina*
Glenview, Illinois

# ITALIAN VENISON ROLLS

Serves: 4
Prep Time: 1 hour

| | |
|---|---|
| 2 **large venison steaks** | 1 **jar Ragu Italian sauce** |
| 8 **oz. mozzarella cheese,** | 6 **T. Worcestershire sauce** |
| **shredded** | ¼ **lb. butter** |
| 1 **lg. onion** | **garlic powder** |
| **fresh mushrooms** | |
| 1 **lg. green pepper** | |

Saute sliced onion, pepper and mushrooms in butter until completely cooked. Remove from pan to drain. Slice steaks ¼-inch thick (it helps if they are partially frozen). Add butter to pan with 6 T. Worcestershire sauce and increase heat. When pan is very hot, sprinkle steaks with garlic and cook 2 minutes on each side. Remove from pan, place ⅓ cup of the vegetable mix and ¼ cup mozzarella cheese on one end of each steak. Roll each steak from that end. Place rolls in a lightly greased baking dish. Pour Ragu sauce over steaks, sprinkle remaining cheese on top. Cover and bake at 350 degrees for 30 minutes. Serve with noodles.

*Randy Moore*
Fairlee, Vermont

## VENISON CHEESEBURGER PIE

Serves: 4
Prep Time: 1 hour

Pie crust (single)
1 lb. ground venison
½ lb. hot sausage
1 tsp. salt
½ tsp. oregano
¼ tsp. pepper

½ cup dry bread crumbs
1 8 oz. can tomato sauce
¼ cup onion, chopped
¼ cup green pepper, chopped
fresh tomato, diced

Heat oven to 425 degrees. Prepare pie crust for 9-inch pie. In skillet, brown meat, drain. Stir in salt, oregano, pepper, crumbs, tomato sauce, onion, tomato and green pepper. Pour in shell. Mix a cheese topping of:

1 egg
¼ cup milk
½ tsp. salt
Worcestershire sauce
2 cup shredded cheese

Pour over meat and bake for 30 minutes.

*Keith Dixon*
Niehoopany, Pennsylvania

## FRIED VENISON MEAT LOAF

Serves: 6
Prep Time: 20 minutes

1 lb. ground venison
salt and pepper
1 egg
2 dashes Worcestershire

1 onion, finely chopped
¼ green pepper, chopped
22 Ritz crackers, crushed
½ cup milk

Mix all ingredients well. Form into hamburger patties. Brown
in a skillet with hot oil. Excellent when topped with chili sauce,
catsup or steak sauce.

*John Zanon*
Norway, Michigan

## FRIED VENISON STEAK

Serves: 2-4
Prep Time: 30 minutes

1 lb. steak
1 egg, beaten
1 tsp. garlic salt
salt and pepper

1½ cups bread crumbs
1½ tsp. parsley flakes
½ cup Parmesan cheese

Combine bread crumbs, parsley, garlic salt, Parmesan cheese,
salt and pepper. Dip steak in egg, then in bread mixture. Fry
covered, for about 20 to 30 minutes.

*Ronald Bowers*
Sugar Grove, West Virginia

## MARINATED VENISON

Serves: varies
Prep Time: 12 hours

**venison steaks**
**1  bottle beer**
**½  cup soy sauce**

**1  tsp. garlic salt**
**1  tsp. onion powder**

Combine all ingredients. Pour over sliced venison. Marinate
overnight. Flour and fry venison steaks in hot fat or oil until
cooked.

*Mary Beth Kibler*
Kibler Outfitter & Guide Service
Box A-6
Sand Springs, MT 59077

## VENISON SCALLOPINI

Serves: 4
Prep Time: 1 hour

**½  cup oil**
**1  lb. venison**
**2  onions**
**1  can mushrooms**
**salt and pepper**

**½  tsp. garlic powder**
**1  can tomato paste**
**1  tsp. oregano**
**white wine**
**12  oz. mozzarella cheese**

Marinate thinly sliced venison strips in wine overnight. In large
skillet, saute onions in oil until tender. Add venison, garlic, salt
and pepper. Brown on both sides. Add oregano. Cook for 15
minutes, until tender. Add tomato paste. Simmer, covered, for
20-25 minutes. Slice mozzarella cheese thin and place strips on
venison. Cover skillet for additional time to melt cheese.

*Joe Vita*
Stamford, Connecticut

## STEAKS LA PAN

Serves: 6-8
Prep Time: 6½-7 hours

4 lbs. venison steak
¾ cup olive oil
1 cup onion, chopped
¼ cup pimento, chopped
1 T. parsley flakes
1 tsp. celery seed

2 cans mushroom steak sauce
1 cup white wine
1 T. soy sauce
dash of hot sauce
1 clove garlic, chopped
3 tsp. salt

Place olive oil in Dutch oven. Cut steaks into serving size pieces and brown in oil. Add other ingredients and mix well. Cook on low heat for 6 hours or until meat is well done. Serve over rice or small noodles.

*Bobby Wright*
Highland, Indiana

## FINGER STEAKS

Serves: 2-4
Prep Time: 15 minutes

antelope, deer or elk steaks
seasoned salt
hickory salt
onion powder

garlic powder
flour
pepper

Pound steaks to tenderize and cut into 2-inch by 1-inch strips. Dredge in mixture of all ingredients. Put into a deep fat fryer until meat is done.

*Vincent Duck*
Faith, South Dakota

# SASKATCHEWAN VENISON

Serves: 4-6
Prep Time: 3 days

| | |
|---|---|
| 4 lbs. venison | 8 T. butter |
| 1½ cups red wine vinegar | flour |
| ½ cup dry red wine | cooking oil |
| 2 carrots, sliced | 1 T. sugar |
| 2 onions, sliced | gingersnaps |
| your favorite spices | |

Mix vinegar, wine, carrot and onions. Pour over meat and marinate for 3 days in the refrigerator. Turn every once in a while to absorb the flavors.

Take meat out of refrigerator and pat dry with paper towels. Do not throw out marinade. Brown meat in 4 T. butter and cook oil in Dutch oven, sprinkling meat with flour as it is turned. Heat the marinade, pour over meat, cover and simmer for about 3 hours until tender. Strain off liquid and skim fat. Melt 4 T. butter, blend in same amount of flour, 1 T. sugar and cooking liquid. Stir until smooth and thickened. Add about a capful of crushed gingersnaps and pour over the meat. Cook slowly for another ½ hour.

*Glen Hill*
Saskatchewan River Hunting Camps
129 First St. E.
Saskatoon, Saskatchewan S7H 1R6

## VENISON EUGENE

Serves: 2
Prep Time: 10 minutes

1 lb. venison steak
4 T. butter
1 small onion, diced
2 T. dry sherry
2 T. brandy

1 T. Worcestershire
3 T. A-1 steak sauce
1 T. chopped chives
1 T. chopped parsley
salt and pepper

Cook onion in 2 T. butter until soft, not brown. Pound steak and sear over high heat in butter and onion, about 2 minutes on each side. Add sherry, A-1 sauce, 2 T. butter, Worcestershire, chives, parsley, pepper and salt. Turn heat to high for 4 minutes. Add brandy and flame. When flame goes out serve with rice and vegetables.

*Eugene Powell*
Greenbelt, Maryland

## GLORIFIED CHOPS

Serves: 8
Prep Time: 30 minutes

8 deer chops
2 lg. onions
4 green peppers
3 cans tomato soup

3 soup cans water
2 cups Minute Rice
salt and pepper

Lay chops on bottom of large roaster. Slice a thick layer of onions on top. Cut green peppers in half and put on top of onion. Fill each green pepper with rice. Pour tomato sauce all around and put a couple spoonfuls on top of rice. Bake at 325 degrees for 3 to 4 hours.

*Haven Post*
Sturgis, Michigan

## CRAZY MAN STEW

Serves: 3-4
Prep Time: 1½ hours

1 venison steak or tenderloin
1 16 oz. can mixed vegetables
1 small onion, diced
1½ tomatoes, diced
¼ cup vegetable oil
1 T. butter
dash cinnamon
dash apple pie spice
dash paprika
garlic salt
salt and pepper

Dice meat. In slow cooker, brown meat on all sides in vegetable oil and butter. Dice onion and tomatoes into cooker. Add mixed vegetables and spices. Let simmer for 1½ hours at 180 degrees. Stir and add water as needed.

*Steven Harding*
Green Mountain, North Carolina

## HUNTER'S STEW SOUP

Serves: 8
Prep Time: 3 hours

1 lb. venison
1 rabbit
1 squirrel
2 qts. water
1 can corn
1 can mixed vegetables
¼ cup potatoes, cubed
2 tsp. beef base
1 tsp. black pepper
1 tsp. celery salt
1 T. chopped onion
¼ cup rice
2 cups tomatoes, diced
salt

Cut all the meat into cubes. Place in large pan with remaining ingredients. Cook for 1 hour, then simmer for 1 hour.

*Charles Smith*
Plattsburgh, New York

## NO-PEEK CASSEROLE

Serves: 8
Prep Time: 8 hours

2 lbs. stew meat
flour
oil
2 cups water

2 cups dark red sherry
1 can mushroom soup
1 pkg. onion soup mix

Brown meat in oil and drain. Put in 4-quart casserole. Stir together the water, sherry, mushroom soup and onion soup mix. Pour over meat and stir. Cover and bake at 250 degrees for 6 to 8 hours. Stir when opened. Serve over rice or mashed potatoes.

*Haven Post*
Sturgis, Michigan

## APPETIZER TO CASSEROLE IN ONE

Serves: varies
Prep Time: 30 minutes

any game meat
sliced bacon
1 tsp. black pepper

2 cups water
½ cup Worcestershire

Cut meat into cubes and wrap each in ½ slice bacon. Secure with toothpicks. Mix remaining ingredients in cast iron skillet and broil meat in mixture until tender and most of the liquid is gone. Brown by stirring in hot grease left in pan. Makes great hors d'oeuvres. For casserole, cut meat, chop bacon and cook as above. Then stir in a can of sliced potatoes and a can of any vegetable. Heat thoroughly.

*Shelly Amys*
Poplar, Wisconsin

## MILD MEXICAN BARBEQUE

Serves: 20-40
Prep Time: 1 hour

| | |
|---|---|
| 1½ cup chopped onion | ¾ cup chopped celery |
| 3 T. margarine | ⅓ cup plus 1 T. lemon juice |
| 6 lbs. ground venison | 2 T. plus 1 tsp. wine vinegar |
| 2 15 oz. cans tomato puree | ⅓ cup packed sugar |
| 1 16 oz. can tomato paste | ½ tsp. red cayenne pepper |
| 1 16 oz. can water | ½ tsp. cumin seed |

Brown onion in margarine and add venison. Brown venison,
drain and add remaining ingredients, crushing cumin seeds
first. Simmer for 45 minutes. Fills 40 large hamburger buns.
This may be frozen.

*Michael Wagner*
Rockport, Illinois

## BARBEQUE DEER LOIN

Serves: 4
Prep Time: 1 hour

| | |
|---|---|
| 1 venison tenderloin | vegetable oil |
| 2 green peppers | barbeque sauce |
| 2 onions | salt and pepper |

Cut tenderloin into steak size pieces. Brown in hot oiled skillet.
Cover with barbeque sauce and let simmer. When about half
done, add sliced peppers and onions. Salt and pepper to taste.
(Venison steak may be substituted for tenderloin.)

*Lee Redifer*
Bridgewater, Virginia

# BARBEQUED MEATBALLS

Serves: 4
Prep Time: 1 hour

| | |
|---|---|
| 1 lb. ground venison | garlic powder |
| ½ cup bread crumbs | onion powder |
| 1 egg | 1 pkg. onion soup mix |
| ½ cup water | ½ cup catsup |
| 1 tsp. salt | ½ cup brown sugar |
| ¼ tsp. pepper | ½ cup water |

Mix first 8 ingredients together and form meatballs. Brown in pan with oil. Mix together remaining ingredients, heat in casserole dish. Add meatballs and bake ½ hour.

*Glen Hill*
Saskatchewan River Hunting Camps
129 First St.E.
Saskatoon, Saskatchewan S7H 1R6

# JOE'S BARBEQUED DEER

Serves: 4-6
Prep Time: 3 hours

| | |
|---|---|
| 1 venison roast | 1 lg. green pepper |
| salt and pepper | 1 qt. barbeque sauce |
| 2 onions | 2 cups rice |

Cut roast into chunk size pieces. Stew meat for 2 hours with onion, salt and pepper. Drain stock except for 1 cup, and barbeque sauce and diced green pepper. Cook on low for 1 hour. Cook rice. Pour stew over rice.

*Joe Sneed*
Gastonia, North Carolina

## RAE'S ZESTY MEAT AND RICE

Serves: 4-6
Prep Time: 1 hour

- 2 **lbs. wild game meat**
- 2 **cups barbeque sauce**
- ¼ **tsp. garlic salt**
- 4 **tsp. onion, chopped**
- 1 **cup water**

Brown meat. Mix barbeque sauce, water, onion and garlic.
Pour over meat and bring to a boil for 3 minutes, then simmer
for 45 minutes. Serve over rice or noodles.

*LeRoy Ferguson*
Jonesville, Michigan

## VENISON SAUSAGE

Yield: 25 pounds
Prep Time: 1 hour

| | | | |
|---|---|---|---|
| 15 | lbs. ground venison | 3 | tsp. mace |
| 10 | lbs. ground pork | 2 | tsp. allspice |
| 9 | tsp. garlic salt | ¾ | tsp. nutmeg |
| 9 | tsp. black pepper | ¼ | cup salt |
| 3 | tsp. crushed red pepper | 2 | tsp garlic powder |

Grind venison and pork together. Spread meat out over a clean table and add all spices. Mix together with your hands. You can then refrigerate the sausage for a few hours if you wish. Put in casings or freeze it bulk.

*John Zanon*
Norway, Michigan

## VENISON SAUSAGE

Yield: 8 lbs.
Prep Time: 1 hour

| | | | |
|---|---|---|---|
| 5 | lbs. ground venison | | garlic cloves, ground |
| 1 | lb. ground pork | 2 | T. sage |
| 2 | lbs. ground beef | 2 | tsp. celery salt |
| 1 | cup green pepper, ground | 1 | T. Worcestershire |
| ½ | cup onion, ground | 1 | T. red pepper |
| | | 1 | T. black pepper |

Put all ingredients in a bowl and mix together. Bag and fry when needed.

*Charles Smith*
Plattsburgh, New York

## SMOKY VENISON SALAMI

Prep Time: 24 hours

| | |
|---|---|
| 4 lbs. ground venison | 1½ tsp. pepper |
| ¼ cup curing salt | 1½ tsp. garlic powder |
| 2 T. liquid smoke | |

Mix all ingredients and let stand in refrigerator for 24 hours, sealed. Roll out into 2-inch rolls and wrap in foil. Put several small holes in foil, twist ends together and bake at 325 degrees for 1½ to 2 hours to cook out grease. Let cool before freezing.

Note: Place rolls directly on oven racks, with pan underneath to catch grease.

## SPICY VENISON SALAMI

Prep Time: 24 hours

| | |
|---|---|
| 4 lbs. ground venison | 1 tsp. garlic powder |
| ¼ cup curing salt | 2 T. chili powder |
| 3 T. dry white wine | 1 tsp. cumin |

Mix all ingredients. Let stand in refrigerator 24 hours. Roll out into 2-inch rolls and wrap in foil. Put several small holes in foil, twist ends together and bake at 325 degrees for 1½ to 2 hours to cook out grease. Let cool before freezing.

Note: Place rolls directly on oven racks, with pan underneath to catch grease.

*David Sizek*
Ozona, Texas

## VENISON JERKY

Serves: varies
Prep Time: varies

2-3 lbs. venison
1 tsp. meat tenderizer
½ tsp. garlic powder
½ tsp. onion powder
¼ tsp. Tabasco sauce

1 tsp. Heinz 57 sauce
½ tsp. soy sauce
½ tsp. table salt
1 cup cold water

Mix all ingredients in a stainless steel or glass container. Cut venison with the grain into ¼-inch slices and cover with marinade. Refrigerate overnight. Place meat on racks and apply coarse black pepper to taste.

Smoke meat for 2½ to 3 hours with a moderate amount of smoke. If you do not have a smoker, use your oven at the lowest setting possible. (Add liquid smoke to marinade.) Place meat on racks and let dry. Store in a cool, dry place in covered containers.

*Bobby May*
Paragonah, Utah

## JERKY

Serves: 6
Prep Time: 24 hours

liquid smoke
mustard (dry)
garlic powder
pepper

onion powder
soy sauce
meat strips

Cut meat into very thin strips, marinate in mixture for several hours. Hang over line outside, inside a tent of cheesecloth for several hours until dry.

*Pat Jacobson*
Arctic Rivers Guide Service
Box 1313
Kodiak, AK 99615

## ANTELOPE STEAKS SUPREME

Serves: 3
Prep Time: 1 hour

| | | | |
|---|---|---|---|
| 3 | round steaks | | salt and pepper |
| 2 | tsp. salt | | garlic salt |
| ¼ | cup vinegar | | onion salt |
| 1 | bay leaf | 1 | can cream of mushroom soup |
| 1 | clove garlic | 1 | can water |

Put steaks in shallow pan with water to cover. Add salt, vinegar, bay leaf and garlic. Soak 3 to 4 hours. Remove steaks, drain, sprinkle with seasonsings. Dredge in flour. Heat oil in skillet, brown meat, cover. Simmer 40 minutes. Add soup and water and simmer 20 minutes longer.

*Karen Wood*
Elko, Nevada

# MOOSE MEATLOAF

Serves: 6
Prep Time: 1 hour

    2   lbs. ground moose
    1   pkg. onion soup mix
1 ½   cups evaporated milk
    1   T. Worcestershire
    ¼   tsp. pepper
    ½   tsp. garlic salt
Sauce:
    1   10 oz. can tomato soup
    1   T. Worcestershire
    1   T. lemon juice
    1   T. brown sugar

Combine meat ingredients and shape into loaf. Bake at 375 degrees for ½ hour. Combine sauce ingredients and pour over meatloaf. Bake an additional ½ hour.

*Toddy Watson*
Christina Falls Outfitters
Box 6640
Ft. St. John, British Columbia VIJ 4J1

# BLACK BEAR SPAGHETTI SAUCE

Yield: 24 servings
Prep Time: 3½ hours

- 2  **lbs. ground bear**
- 2  **28 oz. cans tomatoes**
- 2  **5½ oz. cans tomato paste**
- 2  **large onions, diced**
- 1  **green pepper, diced**
- 1  **10 oz. can mushrooms, drained**
- 1  **clove garlic, crushed**
   **salt and pepper**
   **oregano**
   **bay leaves**
- ½  **tsp. chili powder**
- 2  **T. Worcestershire**
- 1  **tsp. cornstarch**

Brown meat in frying pan. Drain off excess fat. In a large pot, put canned tomatoes (mashed up), tomato paste, onions, green pepper, mushrooms and garlic. Stir. Add bear meat. Stir. Add remaining spices and stir. Let simmer for 3 hours with no lid. Half way through add cornstarch to thicken. Stir occasionally. Serve with your favorite pasta.

*Kris & Karen Fielding*
Black Ghost Outfitters
1749 Paris St. #309
Sudbury, Ontario P3E 4V4

## BLACK BEAR ROAST

Serves: 4-6
Prep Time: 4¼ hours

  1 **bear roast**
  1 **pkg. onion soup mix**
  1 **can sliced mushrooms**

Remove all fat from roast and wash well. Place on a piece of
heavy foil. Sprinkle package of onion soup mix and can of
mushrooms over roast. Seal tightly and bake in a 350 degree
oven for 4 hours or until very well done. The juice from the
meat will make an excellent gravy base.

*Vera Schmidt*
The Driftwood
R.R. 1 Box 260A
Patten, ME 04765

## CHAR-BROILED BARBEQUE BEAR RIBS

Serves: 4-6
Prep Time: varies

  1 **side of bear ribs**           **honey**
    **your favorite barbeque**      **butter**
    **sauce**                       **your favorite seasonings**

Cut the ribs into desired size. Season well on both sides, cover
and refrigerate for 1 to 12 hours, to absorb the seasoning.
When grill is ready, put the ribs on the grill, adding slices of
butter to each chuck of ribs. Turn often, adding butter with
each turn. When ribs are almost ready, prepare a barbeque
sauce using ¾ of your favorite sauce and ¼ honey. Brush on
sauce, let sit a while, then brush on other side.

*John Zanon*
Norway, Michigan

# BEAR STROGANOFF

Serves: 4-6
Prep Time: 30-45 minutes

- 2 cups cubed bear meat
- ½ cup onion
- ¼ cup butter, unsalted
- 1 tsp. salt
- 2 T. flour
- ¼ tsp. pepper
- 1 can sliced mushrooms
- 1 can cream of celery soup
- 1 cup dairy sour cream
- 1 clove garlic
- 4 cups egg noodles

Saute onions in butter. Add bear meat and brown. Make sure onions are tender and bear is well done. Stir in flour, salt, garlic, pepper and mushrooms. Cook five minutes, stirring constantly over medium-low heat. Stir in soup, heat to boiling, stirring constantly. Add a little water if necessary. Reduce heat, simmer uncovered 10 minutes. Prepare egg noodles. Stir in sour cream and heat through. Serve over bed of noodles.

*Frank Whitley*
Eureka, California

## BARBEQUED LION RIBS

Serves: 4
Prep Time: 3 hours

4 lbs. lion ribs
onion, diced
salt and pepper

Barbeque Sauce:
1 cup catsup
¼ cup sugar
3 T. vinegar
1 T. Worcestershire

Place lion ribs in covered baking pan. Add salt, pepper and diced onions. Pour barbeque sauce over ribs and bake for 2 hours at 325 degrees. Turn ribs every 15 minutes.

*Una Earl*
Golden Bear Outfitters
Box 348 Star Rt.
Judith Gap, MT 59453

## PORCUPINE AND PINEAPPLE SHISH KABOBS

Serves: 2-4
Prep Time: 20 minutes

2-4 rear porcupine legs
2 lg. pineapple rings
¼ cup pineapple juice

Alternate the porcupine legs and pineapple chunks on skewers. Let the legs cook a bit, then brush on the pineapple juice. Cook until done.

*Anthony Pace*
Fort Kent, Maine

# FRIED ALLIGATOR

Serves: 4
Prep Time: 20 minutes

| | |
|---|---|
| 1 lb. alligator meat | 1 tsp. salt |
| 1 can beer | 1 tsp. pepper |
| ½ cup flour | corn meal |
| 1 tsp. Season-All | oil |

Slice meat into finger strips. Mix beer, flour, Season-all, salt and pepper to form a batter. Coat alligator meat with batter and dredge with corn meal. Fry in hot oil until golden brown.

# ALLIGATOR MEATBALLS

Serves: 4
Prep Time: 30 minutes

| | |
|---|---|
| 1 lb. alligator meat | 2 tsp. lemon pepper |
| 1 egg | ½ tsp. salt |
| 2 T. onion, finely chopped | ¼ cup bread crumbs |
| 2 T. celery, finely chopped | flour |
| 1 T. parsley flakes | 1 cup cooking oil |
| 2 T. shallots, chopped | |

Chop or grind alligator meat. Combine all ingredients except flour and oil, and allow to set for 1 hour. Form into 1-inch balls, dredge with flour and fry in oil until brown. Serve hot. For added flavor, dredge meatballs in mustard before dredging in flour.

*Thomas Fletcher*
Mathews, Louisiana

## COYOTE SOUP

Serves: 6
Prep Time: 4 hours

        coyote hind quarter
    3 onions, chopped
    2 heads of cabbage, chopped
    8 potatoes, chopped
    2 cups red wine
        garlic
        salt and pepper
        spices

Cut meat into chunks and brown in oil. Add onion, garlic and your other favorite spices. Cook for ½ hour, then add cabbage and potatoes. Cook until tender. Serve with hot biscuits.

*Henry Johnson*
Trinidad, Colorado

## CHILI COOKOFF!

The ICS's annual Chili Cookoff draws huge crowds each year.

Chili may well be the ultimate outdoors, in-the-woods, camping-type food. It can be prepared ahead of time and brought to camp for a quick heat and eat meal or it can be prepared in camp to simmer all day over an open fire. Just about any ingredient, including wild game has been put into chili, and it always comes out tasting great! Above all else, that's what makes chili a truly wonderful food—everybody loves it!

When we decided to include chili in this year's NAHC Wild Game Cookbook, we remembered the adage, "If you want the best, go to the source!" That's why we went to the folks at the International Chili Society. They are the "keepers of the key" when it comes to making and eating fine chili!

The purpose of the Society is to develop and improve the preparation and appreciation of true chili and to determine each year the World Champion Chili Cook. Along the way, the Society raises lots of money for charity and has a ball doing it!

The ICS's big event each year is the World Championship Chili Cookoff held annually since 1979, and draws huge crowds of up to 15,000 eager chili lovers. In 1985, the prize money for the World Championship totalled $35,000, with $25,000 of that going to 1985 World Champion Carol Hancock for her "Shotgun Willie Chili"!

By including International Chili Society recipes in this year's NAHC Wild Game Cookbook, we hope you'll find pleasure in preparing and eating your own versions of these recipes. The ICS pulled together these interesting facts on chili preparation in the United States. Enjoy this bit of trivia while you're waiting for your chili to simmer.

Bon appetit! (In chili talk that's "grab a bowl and dig in!")

## CHILI FACTS

The following facts were compiled pertaining to chili cooked from scratch in the United States. Percentages relate to an estimated 75,000,000 households.

**CHILI REGION**

|  | Total U.S. | Northeast | North Central | South | West |
|---|---|---|---|---|---|
| Homemade Chili ever prepared | 66.8% | 48.2% | 78.9% | 68.0% | 70.1% |
| Homemade chili average per month | 1.4% | 1.3% | 1.5% | 1.5% | 1.2% |

66.8% based on 75,000,000 households means that 50,100,000 people cooked homemade chili in the United States. We estimate that from 12,000 to 15,000 people have competed in a chili cookoff in the last 5 years and the number is growing.

So if you like chili—to cook it and eat it—you're not alone. For more information about the International Chili Society, contact them at: I.C.S., P.O. Box 2566, Newport Beach, CA 92663.

**BASIL** Dried or fresh, the flavor is reminiscent of mint and cloves combined. It is good in almost any dish containing tomatoes, since it seems to sweeten them.

**BAY LEAF** Dried or fresh, used sparingly, it is quite strong. The aromatic and slightly bitter flavor enhances meat, fish, poultry, soups and sauces.

**CAYENNE** is a member of the Capsicum family. The pepper is ground, mixed with yeast and flour and baked into a hard cake. After regrinding, it appears on your grocery shelf as a super spice.

**CILANTRO** Dried or fresh, it is a great flavor-enhancer in Mexican and Chinese cooking. Cilantro is the parsley-like leaf of fresh coriander.

**CORIANDER** seeds, when dried, have a sweet taste reminiscent of lemon peel and sage combined.

**CUMIN** seed is similar to caraway seed in flavor and appearance, however, it is lighter in color and the flavor is stronger and less refined. Also comes in powdered form.

**GARLIC** is one of the most common spices, included in almost every recipe except ice cream. Garlic, either fresh cloves, powder or salt, is a necessity to the chili chef.

**OREGANO** is a wild marjoram whose taste is sharper and spicier than marjoram's. It is a common ingredient in Spanish and Mexican foods.

**PAPRIKA** is a mild, powdered seasoning made from sweet red peppers. Used extensively as a flavor and color enhancing additive.

# CAROL HANCOCK'S SHOTGUN WILLIE CHILI
## 1985 World Championship Chili Recipe

Serves: 6-8
Prep Time: 3½ hours

|  |  |
|---|---|
| 6 | lbs. prime beef, cubed or coarse ground |
| 4 | medium onions, finely chopped |
| 1 | 15 oz. can Hunts tomato sauce |
| 6 | New Mexico dried pepper pods |
| 6 | pasilla dried pods |
| 4 | cups beef broth |
| 2 | T. vinegar |
| 1 | tsp. Tabasco |
| 16 | T. Gebhardt's Chili Powder |
| 2 | T. ground cumin |
| 1 | tsp. cayenne |
| 1 | T. monosodium glutamate |
| ½ | tsp. sugar |
| 14 | garlic pods, chopped |
| 1 | cup water |
| 1½ | T. oregano leaves |
| 2-3 | T. Wesson oil |
|  | salt and pepper |

Remove stems and seeds from pepper pods. Boil peppers in water for approximately 1 hour, until pulp separates from skin. Scrape pulp from skin, mash into a paste. Use 1½ cups of this paste in recipe. In the 1 cup of water, bring the 1½ T. oregano leaves to a boil, steep like tea. Strain, add the strained liquid to chili mixture.

Brown beef, a small batch at a time in hot oil, adding onions and black pepper to each batch. Remove meat to chili pot as it browns. Add remaining ingredients, blending well. Cover and simmer 2 hours, stirring occasionally.

## JANET GUTHRIE'S INDIANAPOLIS CHILI

Serves: 8
Prep Time: 2½ hour

  2  lbs. pork sausage, ground
  2  lbs. ground beef
  3  medium onions, minced
  ½  cup green peppers, chopped
  1  4 oz. can green chiles, chopped
  6  medium mushrooms, sliced
  4  lg. tomatoes, peeled and chopped
  4  6 oz. cans tomato paste
  4  15½ oz. cans beef consomme
  3  16 oz. cans refried beans
  1  tsp. Tabasco
  1  tsp. celery seed
  ½  tsp. grated lemon rind
  ½  tsp. pepper
  2  tsp. oregano leaves
  1  2½ oz. can chili powder
     salt

Brown sausage, beef, onions and green peppers in a large
skillet, a little at a time. Place browned meats, vegetables and
spices in a large pot. Add the chiles and remaining ingredients
to the pot and stir until all are well blended. Cook 2 hours,
covered, stirring often to prevent sticking.

# PERRY COMO'S FAVORITE CHILI

Serves: 6
Prep Time: 1¼ hours

    2  T. salad oil
    1  medium onion, chopped
    1  clove garlic, crushed
    1  lb. ground round
    2  tsp. salt
    1  tsp. paprika
    2  tsp. chili powder
    2  16 oz. cans kidney beans
    ½  cup bean liquid
    1  16 oz. can seasoned stewed tomatoes
    1  6 oz. can tomato paste
    ½  tsp. sugar
    ¾  tsp. Tabasco
    1  12 oz. can whole kernel corn, drained

Heat oil in large skillet. Add onions and garlic and cook until
yellow, not brown. Add beef, sprinkle with salt, paprika and
chili powder. Cook meat until brown, breaking up with fork.
Drain kidney beans. Stir in bean liquid, tomatoes, tomato
paste, sugar and Tabasco. Cover and simmer 30 minutes. Add
kidney beans and corn, simmer 15 minutes stirring
occasionally.

# FESTUS' (KEN CURTIS) GUNSMOKE CHILI

Serves: 8-10
Prep Time: 3½ hours

- 4 lbs. coarse ground venison or lean beef
- 2 lg. onions, minced
- 2 tsp. monosodium glutamate
- 1½ tsp. salt
- 1 tsp. ground black pepper
- 2 T. parsley flakes
- 1 tsp. Season-All
- 1½ tsp. basil leaves, crushed by hand
- 1½ tsp. oregano leaves, crushed by hand
- 1 tsp. cayenne
- 4 T. chili powder
- 4 cups bouillon
- 4 cups tomato sauce

Mince the meat fine with a fork while browning. Add remaining ingredients in a large iron pot. Stir all together and simmer for 2½ to 3 hours.

## LADY BIRD JOHNSON'S PEDERNALES RIVER SPECIAL CHILI

Serves: 8-10
Prep Time: 1½ hours

- 4 lbs. chopped chili meat, venison or beef
- 1 lg. onion, chopped
- 2 cloves garlic, minced
- 1 tsp. oregano
- 1 tsp. cumin powder
- 2 T. chili powder
- 2 12 oz. cans tomatoes
  salt
- 2 cups hot water

Put meat, onion and garlic into a large skillet and sear until lightly browned. Add all other ingredients. Bring to a boil. Lower heat, cover and simmer 1 hour. Skim off grease and serve hot.

## JAMES GARNER'S OKLAHOMA CHILI
## Known in Oklahoma as "Sooner" Chili

Serves: 6-8
Prep Time: 3½ hour

- 2  lbs. ground chuck
- 2  medium onions, chopped
- 2  bell peppers, chopped
- 2  hot, yellow peppers, chopped
- 2  16 oz. cans whole tomatoes, chopped
- ½  tsp. garlic salt
- 2  tsp. salt
- ½  tsp. black pepper
- 4  tsp. chili powder
- 2  tsp. brown sugar
- ½  cup honey
- ¼  lb. margarine
- 1  tsp. Tabasco

Brown meat lightly in skillet and transfer to a large pot. Saute onions and peppers in skillet and add them to meat. Saute tomatoes and add to meat mixture. Add seasonings and blend well. Simmer for 3 hours in covered pot, stirring often.

## VEGETABLE CHILI
### For the few who secretly prefer vegetable soup to chili

Serves: 6
Prep Time: 3½ hours

2 lbs. ground beef
1 cup onion, chopped
2 green peppers, chopped
2 stalks celery, chopped
2 cloves garlic, minced
1 10 oz. can tomato juice
1 16 oz. can tomatoes, chopped

1 16 oz. can kidney beans
½ tsp. parsley
¼ tsp. saffron
¼ tsp. rosemary
1 tsp. salt
¼ tsp. pepper
1 T. Tabasco

Saute beef, onion, peppers, celery and garlic together until onions and peppers are tender. Cover and simmer for 1 hour. Add remaining ingredients and cook 3 hours. Add water until desired consistency is reached.

## BOSTON CHILI
### A very mild blend, featuring eggplant.

Serves: 4
Prep Time: 2½ hours

1½ lb. ground beef
4 cups water
2 16 oz. cans kidney beans
1 28 oz. can tomatoes, undrained
1 6 oz. can tomato paste
1 small eggplant, peeled and cubed

½ green pepper, chopped
1 lg. onion, minced
2 T. chili powder
1 tsp. salt
½ tsp. pepper

Brown meat in a large skillet. Crumble into small pieces. Add remaining ingredients, simmer 2 hours, stirring occasionally.

## CINCINNATI CHILI
## One of the most famous of all chili recipes

Serves: 6
Prep Time: overnight

      1  qt. beef broth
      2  lbs. ground beef
    ¼  cup onion flakes
      4  T. chili powder
      1  tsp. ground cinnamon
      1  tsp. ground cumin
    ¾  tsp. instant minced onions
    ½  tsp. salt
    ¼  tsp. ground allspice
    ¼  tsp. ground cloves
    ¼  tsp. ground red pepper
      1  bay leaf
      1  15 oz. can tomato sauce
      2  T. cider or white vinegar
    ½  oz. unsweetened chocolate

Boil beef broth in a 4-quart saucepan. Slowly add beef to broth
until meat separates into small pieces. Cover and simmer 30
minutes. Add remaining ingredients. Mix well. Bring to a boil.
Reduce heat, simmer, covered, 1 hour, stirring occasionally.
Refrigerate overnight. Skim off fat before heating and serving.

## TEXAS RED
## If there were but one name for chili, it would be "Texas Red."

Serves: 6
Prep Time: 3 hours

- 3 lbs. round steak
- ¼ lb. suet
- 1 T. Mexican oregano
- 1 3 oz. bottle chili powder
- 1 T. cayenne
- 1 T. cumin seed, crushed
- 1 clove garlic, minced
- 1 T. Tabasco
- 6 medium tomatoes, chopped
- 6 jalapeno peppers, chopped
- 2 quarts water
- 4 T. masa flour (mix with 2 T. water to make a paste)

Cut steak into ¼-inch cubes. In heavy pot, brown together the steak and suet until redness is gone from meat. Add oregano, chili powder, cayenne, cumin seed, garlic and Tabasco. Mix well. Add tomatoes, jalapenos, and enough water for desired consistency. Simmer, uncovered, for 2 hours, stirring frequently. Skim off fat, add masa flour paste and simmer for 45 minutes, adding more water if necessary.

## CHILI COLORADO
## Mashing the beans hides them from the purist!

Serves: 4
Prep Time: 1½ hours

      2  lbs. steak
      3  T. corn oil
      1  medium onion, minced
      4  cloves garlic, minced
      2  tsp. salt
      2  T. cumin powder
      5  T. chili powder
      2  T. masa flour
      2  tsp. brown sugar
      1  16 oz. can kidney beans, mashed
      1  16 oz. can tomatoes, undrained and squeezed
      1  6 oz. can tomato paste

Cut meat into ¼-inch cubes and saute in corn oil. Remove from skillet and set aside. Add onion, garlic, salt, cumin, chili powder and masa flour to oil and blend until smooth. Add brown sugar, kidney beans, tomatoes and tomato paste, stirring until all ingredients are well blended. Add meat and stir again. Cover, stirring frequently, for 1 hour.

## OUTBACK (AUSTRALIAN) CHILI
This recipe is supposed to have been developed by a couple of Australian tennis players while in California, but is now popular Down Under.

Serves: 6
Prep Time: 2½ hours

```
 3  lbs. kangaroo meat
¼   cup coconut oil
 1  cup onion, minced
 2  cloves garlic, minced
 4  T. cumin seed
 1  tsp. salt
 2  tsp. paprika
 1  cup bamboo shoots
½   tsp. white pepper
 2  lbs. cherry tomatoes, quartered
 2  10½ oz. cans beef bouillon
 1  tsp. dry mustard
```

Cut kangaroo meat into ¼-inch cubes. In a very large pot, brown meat in oil until golden brown. Add remaining ingredients and stir thoroughly. Bring quickly to a boil, reduce heat and slowly cook for 2 hours or until meat breaks apart easily.

Note: Pork may be substituted if kangaroo meat is unavailable, but then you have to change the name of the dish!

## GOOBER PEA CHILI
### Originated in Alabama, not Georgia, where peanuts are called Goober Peas.

Serves: 6
Prep Time: 2 hours

     2  lbs. fatty ground beef
    ¼  lbs. suet, ground
     1  large green pepper, chopped
     2  lg. onions, chopped
     1  clove garlic, minced
     2  16 oz. cans whole tomatoes, chopped
     4  red hot Italian peppers, chopped
     4  T. chili powder
     2  cups water
     1  cup small Redskin type peanuts

Brown beef in suet and reserve in skillet. In saucepan, add green pepper, onions, garlic, tomatoes, red peppers and chili powder. Cook over medium heat, stirring often, for 15 minutes. Add meat and enough water for desired consistency. Simmer, covered, for 1½ hours, stirring frequently. Add peanuts and cook, uncovered, over low heat for 15 minutes.

## CHILI ORIENTAL
### . . . . combines two diverse cultures.

Serves: 4-6
Prep Time: 2½ hours

- 2 lbs. pork shoulder, cubed
- ½ lb. round steak, cubed
- 2 lg. green peppers, chopped
- 2 lg. onions, chopped
- 2 stalks celery, diced
- 4 cups beef broth
- 1 8 oz. can bamboo shoots
- 1 8 oz. can water chestnuts, sliced
- 1 tsp. pepper
- 2 T. chili powder
- 4 oz. soy sauce
- 3 T. cornstarch
- 1 sm. pkg. bean sprouts
- 8 mushrooms, sliced

Cube meat (do not trim fat from pork). Brown pork and pork fat in large skillet. Add beef and brown with peppers, onions and celery. Cover and simmer 20 minutes, until onions are transparent. Stir frequently. Add beef broth, bamboo shoots, water chestnuts, pepper and chili powder. Blend. Combine soy sauce with cornstarch until smooth. Pour slowly into meat mixture while stirring. Continue stirring until thickened. Add remaining ingredients. Cover, stirring frequently, and simmer 2 hours or until meat is tender.

## CHILI CALIENTE CALIFORNIA
### The cabrito adds a sweet flavor.

Serves: 4-6
Prep Time: 3 hours

- 2 T. beef fat
- 2 cups onions, chopped
- 1 8 oz. can hot chile peppers, minced
- 1 clove garlic, minced
- 2 lbs. cabrito (goat)
- 4 cups tomatoes, chopped
- 1 T. sugar
- 2 tsp. salt
- ¼ cup water
- 3 T. chili powder
- 2 T. A-1 sauce
- 1 16 oz. can kidney beans, with juice
- 2 stalks celery, minced

Cut goat into ¼-inch cubes. Heat fat in a large skillet. Add onions, hot chile peppers, garlic and goat. Brown until onions are tender. Add remaining ingredients, cover and simmer for 2 to 3 hours, depending on desired thickness, stirring occasionally. Add water if mixture is thicker than you desire.

# ITALIAN CHILI

Serves: 6-8
Prep Time: 3 hours

1½  lbs. ground beef
½  lb. pepperoni, ground
½  lb. Italian sausage, ground
2  cups onions, chopped
1  T. garlic, minced
1  lg. eggplant, peeled and cubed
1  cup zucchini, chopped
1  15 oz. can tomato sauce
1  8 oz. can whole tomatoes, chopped
2  tsp. oregano
3  T. chili powder
¼  tsp. thyme
    salt and pepper
½  cup freshly chopped parsley
½  cup Parmesan cheese
½  cup Marsala wine

Brown beef, pepperoni and Italian sausage in a large skillet.
Break meat into small pieces and stir often. Transfer meat to a
large pot and cook at low heat. Reserve drippings in skillet.
Add onion, garlic, eggplant and zucchini to drippings. Saute
until onions are tender. Transfer eggplant mixture to pot with
meat mixture. Add drippings. Add tomato sauce, tomatoes,
oregano, chili powder, thyme, salt and pepper. Simmer for 2
hours, stirring occasionally. Add parsley, Parmesan cheese
and Marsala wine. Cook at medium heat for 30 minutes.

## SHEEPHERDER'S CHILI
### Adapted from an old Montana recipe

Serves: 6-8
Prep Time: 1 hour

- 2 lbs. ground lamb
- 1 cup onions, chopped
- ¾ cup green peppers, chopped
- 2 medium cloves garlic, minced
- 1 28 oz. can tomatoes, chopped
- 1 T. salt
- 1 bay leaf
- 1 T. chili powder
- 2 4 oz. cans Ortega diced green chiles
- 1 16 oz. can pinto beans, drained

Brown lamb in a large skillet until crumbled. Drain. Add onion, green pepper and garlic. Cook until vegetables are tender. Stir in remaining ingredients except beans. Simmer, covered, for 35 minutes, stirring occasionally. Remove cover and add beans. Simmer, uncovered, 10 minutes or until desired consistency. Garnish with sour cream or Monterey Jack cheese, if desired.

## BUFFALO CHILI
## A modern "Old West" Recipe

Serves: 4-6
Prep Time: 3½ hours

- 2 lbs. buffalo
- 2 medium onions, chopped
- 1 green pepper, minced
- 1 T. celery salt
- 1 T. garlic salt
- 1 T. salt
- 3 T. A-1 sauce
- 4 T. apple cider vinegar
- 1 T. Worcestershire
- 2 T. brown sugar
- 2 tsp. chili powder
- 1 tsp. pepper
- 1 tsp. red pepper
- ½ tsp. paprika
- 1 tsp. oregano
- 1 16 oz. can tomato sauce
- 1 12 oz. can tomato paste
- water

Cut meat into ½-inch cubes. Brown meat, onion and green pepper in a large skillet, cooking until vegetables are tender. Add remaining ingredients, cover and simmer for 20 minutes. Stir occasionally. Add 3 to 4 cups water for desired consistency. Cover, simmer for 3 hours or until it suits your fancy.

## DIAMONDBACK CHILI
### Oddly — or alarmingly — rattlesnake is found in many chili recipes

Serves: 6-8
Prep Time: 5-6 hours

2½  lbs. roast beef
 2  cups rattlesnake meat
 ½  cup masa flour
 ¼  cup cornmeal
 1  tsp. salt
 1  tsp. pepper
 1  4 oz. jar chili powder
 2  cups beef suet, ground
 3  onions, chopped
 4  cloves garlic, crushed
 2  T. cumin powder
 1  tsp. oregano
 4  15½ oz. cans beef broth

Cut beef into 1-inch cubes and rattlesnake into ¼-inch cubes.
Combine meats and let stand at room temperature for 2 hours.
Combine masa flour, cornmeal, salt, pepper and chili powder,
blending well. Dredge meat in flour mixture. Render suet at
high heat. Drop several pieces of meat into hot fat, browning
well. Continue until all meat is browned. Remove all meat from
skillet and add onions and garlic to drippings. Saute at low
heat until vegetables are tender. Return meat to skillet and add
beef broth. Add remaining flour to mixture, stir to blend. Simmer 2½ to 3 hours stirring frequently.

## GENERAL ALARM CHILI
## One for the die-hard leather-throats.

Serves: 6-8
Prep Time: 2 hours

- ⅓ lb. suet, chopped
- 3 lbs. beef
- 2 lg. onions, chopped
- 1 clove garlic, minced
- 1 qt. water
- 1 16 oz. can whole tomatoes, chopped
- 1 8 oz. can tomato sauce
- 1 6 oz. can tomato paste
- 6 T. chili powder
- 8 jalapeno peppers, chopped
- 1 7 oz. can diced green chiles
- 2 T. Tabasco
- 1 tsp. cayenne
- ½ cup vinegar
- ¼ cup cornmeal

Cut beef into 1-inch chunks. In large skillet, render suet and discard casing. Add beef chunks, onion and garlic and cook over medium flame until beef has lost its redness. Transfer beef mixture to a large kettle. Add remaining ingredients; stir to mix well. Bring to a boil and reduce heat. Simmer, covered, for 1½ hours, stirring frequently. Skim off enough fat to satisfy taste.

## BUZZARD'S BREATH
## An old chili term for very hot blends.

Serves: 8
Prep Time: 2½ hours

- ¼ lb. suet, ground
- 4 lbs. flank steak
- 3 lg. onions, chopped
- 3 cloves garlic, chopped
- 1 qt. water
- 8 tomatoes, chopped
- 1 6 oz. can tomato paste
- 8 California chili pods, chopped
- 2 T. crushed red pepper seeds
- ½ cup chili powder
  salt to taste
- 2 T. masa flour

Cut steak into ½-inch cubes. Render suet in large skillet and add steak cubes. Cook over medium heat until cubes are brown. To large pot add steak and all remaining ingredients, except masa flour; stir to mix well. Bring to a boil and reduce heat, simmer, uncovered, for 2 hours, stirring often. Make paste of masa flour and stir into chili. Simmer, uncovered for another 15 minutes.

## CACTUS CHILI
**The tequila adds the needles**

Serves: 6-8
Prep Time: 2 hours

- ½ cup flour
- 4 tsp. salt
- ¼ tsp. pepper
- 3 lbs. pork shoulder
- ¼ cup oil
- ¼ cup instant minced onions
- ¼ tsp. instant minced garlic
- 1 cup water
- 1 16 oz. can tomatoes, chopped
- 4 oz. tequila
- 1½ T. chili powder
- 1 tsp. cumin seed, ground
- 2 16 oz. cans kidney beans, drained
- ½ cup golden raisins

Combine flour, 2 tsp. salt and pepper in a large bowl. Cut pork into 1-inch cubes and toss in mixture, coating each piece thoroughly. Shake off excess flour and reserve. Heat oil in a heavy skillet. Brown thoroughly one-thrid of the meat at a time. Combine dried vegetables with water to rehydrate. Add vegetables to pork drippings and brown. Add tomatoes, tequila and stir well. Add chili powder, cumin and reserved flour to tomatoes, blending well. Bring to a boil. Reduce heat, cover and simmer for 1 hour. Add beans and raisins, simmer 10 minutes. Serve over steamed rice garnished with sliced avocado and shredded Cheddar cheese.

## 50,000-WATT CHILI
## . . . . if you like the malty taste of beer.

Serves: 6-8
Prep Time: 3½ hours

    4 lbs. beef shoulder
    3 cans beer
   10 dried chiles, chopped
    1 lg. onion, chopped
    3 cloves garlic, minced
    3 jalapeno peppers, chopped
    1 16 oz. can tomato paste
    1 tsp. salt
    3 T. barbecue sauce
 1½ tsp. oregano
    2 tsp. cumin powder
      water

Cut beef into 2-inch cubes. Place beef in pressure cooker. Add beer. After steam starts to escape, reduce flame to low and cook for 2 hours. Remove meat and shred. Add chiles, onion, garlic and jalapeno peppers. Return lid and cook under pressure 20 minutes. Remove lid and add remaining ingredients. Cook uncovered 1 hour. If mixture is too thick, add ½ to 1 cup water or to desired consistency.

## SAUSALITO CHILI
### The rice and artichoke hearts make this one interesting.

Serves: 4-6
Prep Time: 45 minutes

- ⅓ cup instant minced onions
- ¼ cup sweet pepper flakes
- ½ cup water
- 1 T. oil
- 1 lb. lean ground beef
- 7 tsp. chili powder
- 1 tsp. salt
- ½ tsp. ground black pepper
- ½ tsp. garlic powder
- 1 24 oz. can tomatoes, chopped
- 8 marinated artichoke hearts
- ½ tsp. oregano
- ½ tsp. sugar
- 2 cups hot cooked rice

Cover instant onion and sweet pepper flakes with water for 10 minutes to rehydrate. Heat oil in a large skillet and saute vegetables 3 minutes. Add meat, chili powder, salt, pepper and garlic powder. Stir and cook 5 minutes or until meat loses red color. Add tomatoes and simmer 5 minutes. Stir in artichoke hearts, oregano leaves and sugar. Cook 10 to 15 minutes. Serve over hot cooked rice.

## DANTE'S INFERNO ARMADILLO CHILI
**One of the hot ones.**

Serves: 8
Prep Time: 2½ hours

- ¼ cup salad oil
- 2 lbs. beef stew meat
- 1 lb. armadillo meat (preferably nine-banded armadillo)
- 3 lg. onions, chopped
- 3 cloves garlic, minced
- 1 qt. water
- 1 8 oz. can tomato sauce
- 1 6 oz. can tomato paste
- ½ cup chili powder
- 8 jalapeno peppers, chopped
- 4 chile pods, dried
- 1 T. Tabasco

Cut beef and armadillo into 1-inch cubes. Heat oil in large
saucepan or kettle. Add meat, onion and garlic. Cook until
meat is browned. Add remaining ingredients, stir to mix well.
Bring to a boil and reduce heat. Simmer, uncovered for 2 hours
or until meat is tender. Stir occasionally.

## EYE-OPENER CHILI
**True chili lovers can eat it 'round the clock, so here's an easy breakfast chili.**

Serves: 6
Prep Time: 1 hour

- 2 T. butter
- 1 medium onion, chopped
- 1 tsp. garlic salt
- ¼ tsp. salt
- ½ tsp. oregano leaves, chopped
- 4 lg. tomatoes, peeled and chopped
- ¼ tsp. Tabasco
- 2 T. chili powder
- 1 16 oz. can kidney beans and liquid
- 6 eggs
- 6 corn muffins, split and toasted

In skillet, melt butter. Add onion and garlic and cook until tender. Add salt, oregano, tomatoes, Tabasco, chili powder and kidney beans and simmer for 30 minutes. Break eggs, one at a time, into a cup, being careful not to break yolks, and ease into simmering sauce. Cover and simmer 10 minutes or until eggs are poached. Carefully spoon one egg and ample sauce over each muffin.

## CHOCOLATE CHILI
### May have been why the phrase "Don't knock it until you've tried it" was coined.

Serves: 8
Prep Time: 2¼ hours

> 2 lbs. ground chuck
> 2 lbs. ground pork
> 2 green peppers, chopped
> 1 lg. onion, chopped
> 1 clove garlic, minced
> ¼ cup bacon drippings
> 8 tomatoes, chopped
> ½ tsp. Tabasco
> 4 T. chili powder
> 2 cups water
> 2 1 oz. squares Mexican chocolate (or sweet chocolate with a pinch of cinnamon and ginger), grated

To large pot add ground chuck, pork, green peppers, onion and garlic and cook over medium heat in bacon drippings for 10 minutes. Add tomatoes, Tabasco, chili powder and water. Simmer, uncovered, for 2 hours. Stir in chocolate and serve.

## BAKED CHILI
## Moves chili to the casserole category.

Serves: 4-6
Prep Time: 1 hour

Chili:
- 3 T. suet
- 2 lbs. ground beef
- ⅓ cup green pepper cut in strips
- 1 cup onion, chopped
- 1 T. chili powder
- 1 tsp. salt
- ½ tsp. pepper
- ½ tsp. monosodium glutamate
- 1 bay leaf
- 1 clove garlic, chopped
- 1 16 oz. can kidney beans
- 2 cups tomatoes, chopped

Topping:
- ⅓ cup flour
- 2 tsp. sugar
- ½ tsp. baking powder
- ¾ cup yellow cornmeal
- 1 egg, beaten
- ⅓ cup buttermilk

Melt suet in a large heavy pot. Add meat, peppers, onions, chili powder, salt, pepper, monosodium glutamate, bay leaf and garlic. Brown meat mixture until peppers and onions are tender. Add beans, cover and simmer for 1 hour. Stir occasionally.

Preheat oven to 375 degrees. Combine flour, sugar, baking powder and cornmeal until well blended. In a separate bowl, combine egg and buttermilk. Pour egg mixture over flour mixture and beat until smooth. Let stand for 5 minutes. Pour chili filling into a 9x13-inch pan. Spoon topping over chili and spread to touch sides. Bake for 30 minutes or until cornmeal turns golden.

## MACARONI CHILI
### Called "Chili Mac" in its native Ohio.

Serves: 4-6
Prep Time: 3½ hours

2 lg. onions, chopped
⅓ cup beef suet
2 lbs. ground beef
½ cup macaroni
2 cups beef broth
1 16 oz. can tomatoes, chopped
1 16 oz. can kidney beans

¼ tsp. garlic powder
½ tsp. pepper
1 tsp. paprika
2 T. chili powder
1 tsp. salt

Brown onion with suet in a large skillet. Add ground beef and cook until meat crumbles. Add macaroni, beef broth and tomatoes. Stir well. Add beans, garlic powder, pepper, paprika, chili powder and salt. Cover, simmer at low heat for 3 hours, stirring often. Serve with hot corn bread and a salad.

# RED BEANS AND RICE

Serves: 8
Prep Time: 2½ hours

    1  lb. dried dark beans
    ½  lb. lean salt pork, diced
    1  clove garlic, minced
    2  T. parsley, chopped
    1  tsp. salt
    ½  tsp. Tabasco
    4  cups hot cooked rice

In large saucepan, cover dried beans with water and soak over-night. Simmer, covered, until tender, about 2 hours. Add additional water if necessary. Drain. In small skillet, fry salt pork until crisp and brown. Remove pork and reserve. Pour off about half of fat and add garlic to skillet. Cook for 2 to 3 minutes. Add to drained beans with parsley, salt, Tabasco and reserved salt pork. Heat and serve over rice.

Note: If dried beans are unavailable, substitute kidney beans.

## EMPANADAS
## A Mexican meat pie.

Yield: 50 Empanadas
Prep Time: 2 hours

1½   cups instant minced onion
1½   cups water
⅔   cup olive or salad oil
5   lbs. ground beef
½   can (gallon) No. 10 tomatoes, broken up
1¼   cups raisins or currants
1¼   cups green olives, pitted and chopped
⅔   cups chili powder
3   T. salt
2½   T. paprika
2   T. oregano leaves, crushed
15   hard boiled eggs, chopped
7½   lbs. pie dough

Combine onion and water to rehydrate for 10 minutes. Heat oil in a large skillet until hot. Add onion and beef and brown 5 minutes. Drain excess fat. Stir in tomatoes, raisins, olives, chili powder, salt, paprika and oregano. Cook uncovered, for 5 minutes, stirring occasionally. Remove from heat and stir in eggs, then cool. Divide dough into 50 portions. On a lightly floured board, roll each separately into a 6-inch circle, ⅛-inch thick. Spoon about ⅓ cup meat mixture onto one side of each circle. Moisten edges with water, fold pastry over filling to form a semicircle. Press edges to seal; crimp. Prick tops of pastries to allow steam to escape. If desired, brush tops with egg yolk beaten with water. Place on cookie sheets. Bake in a preheated oven at 400 degrees for 30 minutes or until golden brown. Serve hot.

## SOPAPILLAS
**Can be served as bread, with honey as dessert, or stuffed as a main dish.**

Yield: 36 puffs
Prep Time: 1 hour

    1  pkg. active dry yeast
    ¼  cup water
    1  cup milk
    2  T. shortening
    1  tsp. salt
    2  tsp. sugar
    3  cups flour
    1  tsp. baking powder
       vegetable oil

Dissolved yeast in warm water. Scald milk, add shortening, salt, sugar and allow to cool to lukewarm. Add yeast to milk mixture. Sift flour and baking powder together into a large mixing bowl, making a well in the center. Pour liquid ingredients into the well and work into a dough. Knead until smooth and elastic, about 15 minutes. Cover with wax paper or plastic wrap and set aside for 20 minutes. Roll dough out to about ¼-inch thickness and cut into triangles or squares about 3 inches across. Fry in hot oil (425 degrees) until golden on each side.

## MILD JALAPENO CORNBREAD

Serves: 6
Prep Time: 2 hours

  ½  cup flour
 1½  cups cornmeal
  2  tsp. sugar
  1  tsp. baking soda
  1  tsp. baking powder
 1½  cups buttermilk
  1  tsp. salt
  1  7 oz. can mild jalapeno peppers, chopped
 1½  cups onions, minced
  2  eggs beaten
  1  cup sharp Cheddar cheese
  3  T. bacon drippings

Combine dry ingredients, except salt, in a large bowl. Heat
milk with salt until hot. Add jalapenos and onion, cover and
cook for 30 minutes over low heat. Cool. Mix eggs and cheese.
Blend dry ingredients, liquids, cheese mixture and bacon drippings until smooth. Pour into a well-greased 9-inch square baking pan. Bake at 425 degrees for 40 to 50 minutes.

## JALAPENO GRIDDLE CAKES

Yield: 12 cakes
Prep Time: 30 minutes

  2  cups Bisquick baking mix       2  eggs
  1  small green chile, chopped    ¾  cup buttermilk
  ¼  cup jalapeno peppers, minced

Beat ingredients with a whisk in a small bowl until smooth. Pour
small amounts onto hot griddle, about ¼ cup each, and cook
until slightly thickened. Turn and cook until golden brown.
Serve with butter and honey.

## REFRIED BEAN PIE
**If there's a Texan around, you can't put the beans in the chili, so . . .**

Serves: 4
Prep Time: 2 hours

- **2 cups refried beans**
- **2 eggs, beaten**
- **2 cups sugar**
- **2 T. pumpkin pie spices**
- **1 tsp. vanilla**
- **1 tsp. cornstarch**
- **1 unbaked 9-inch pie shell**

Heat refried beans in a medium saucepan. Slowly add eggs, then the sugar and blend. Add spices, vanilla and cornstarch, stir until well blended. Cool for 30 minutes. Fill pastry shell and bake at 375 degrees for 1 hour.

## BEER PAN BREAD

Serves: 6-8
Prep Time: 45 minutes

- **4 cups Bisquick baking mix**
- **1 tsp. brown sugar**
- **2 tsp. sugar**
- **1 12 oz. can beer**
- **2 T. grease**

Combine Bisquick baking mix, sugars and beer, stirring until thoroughly blended. Pour into a heavily greased iron skillet and cover. Simmer on top of the stove, covered, at low heat for 30 to 35 minutes. Slice while piping hot and serve like corn bread.

## MISSISSIPPI CORNPONE

Serves: 8
Prep Time: 30 minutes

| | |
|---|---|
| 1 cup flour | ¼ cup molasses |
| 1 cup cornmeal | 1 egg |
| 4 tsp. baking powder | 1 cup milk |
| ½ tsp. salt | ¼ cup bacon drippings |

Sift together flour, cornmeal, baking powder and salt in a mixing bowl. Add molasses, egg, milk and bacon drippings, beat until smooth. Bake in a well-greased 8-inch square baking pan at 425 degrees for 20 to 25 minutes.

## CREAMY GUACAMOLE

Yield: 3 cups
Prep Time: 15 minutes

| | |
|---|---|
| 2 ripe avocados | ½ tsp. Worcestershire |
| 2 T. mayonnaise | ¼ tsp. garlic powder |
| 2 drops Tabasco | ½ tsp. seasoning salt |
| 1 T. fresh lime juice | 1 tsp. chili powder |

Peel avocados and work through a sieve or puree in a blender. Add remaining ingredients and blend until smooth. Chill until ready to serve with tortilla chips, as a salad or with nachos.

## RED CHILI SAUCE (SALSA ROJO)

Yield: 3 cups
Prep Time: 1½ hours

2 cups red chiles
2 small onions, chopped
1 clove garlic, minced
2 T. oil

1 cup chicken broth
1 tsp. cumin powder
2 tsp. salt
1 tsp. oregano

Remove seeds and veins from chiles and put in a medium saucepan. Add onions, garlic and oil. Heat until steaming, cover and simmer about 15 minutes at very low heat. Stir frequently to avoid sticking. Add remaining ingredients. Blend well. Continue cooking at very low heat for 60 minutes or until sauce thickens. Stir occasionlly.

## CHILED SOUR CREAM
**Spoon this excellent sour cream-chile sauce into your baked potatoes next time instead of sour cream with chives.**

Yield: 3 cups
Prep Time: 2½ hours

1 7 oz. can green chiles, chopped and drained
¼ tsp. Tabasco
½ tsp. salt
½ tsp. paprika
1 tsp. instant minced onions
1 16 oz. container sour cream

Combine green chiles, Tabasco, salt, paprika and instant minced onions in a small bowl. Let stand 30 minutes to rehydrate onions. Mix well to blend. Fold into sour cream and refrigerate 2 hours before serving.

## MUSTARD-CHILI SALSA

Yield: 2½ cups
Prep Time: overnight

- 1 cup onion, minced
- 2 cloves garlic, minced
- ½ cup butter
- ½ cup green chile salsa
- 1 tsp. dry mustard
- 1 tsp. prepared mustard
- 1 tsp. salt
- ¼ cup minced pimentos

Saute onion and garlic in butter until onions are transparent.
Simmer about 10 minutes. Add remaining ingredients, blend
well, cover and simmer 10 minutes. Cook. Pour into a bowl and
refrigerate overnight for an excellent marinade sauce.

## MEXICAN SALAD DRESSING

Yield: 1¼ cups
Prep Time: several days

¼ tsp. pepper
½ tsp. chili powder
¼ tsp. paprika
½ tsp. dry mustard
¼ tsp. garlic powder
½ tsp. onion powder
½ tsp. salt
⅓ cup vinegar
⅔ cup oil

Place all ingredients in a quart jar and shake vigorously. Store several days, unrefrigerated, before using. Shake frequently during this time.

## SOMBRERO CHILI DIP
## Serve hot with corn chips for dipping.

Serves: 6-8
Prep Time: ½ hour

- 1 lb. ground beef
- ¼ cup onion, minced
- 1 clove garlic, minced
- 1 8 oz. can tomato sauce
- 1 7 oz. can Ortega diced green chiles
- 1 16 oz. can kidney beans, drained and mashed
- 1 tsp. salt

Garnish:
- ½ cup grated Longhorn cheese
- ¼ cup ripe olives, pitted and sliced
- ¼ cup onion, chopped

Brown beef in a large skillet until crumbled. Drain. Add onion and garlic and saute until onion is tender. Mix in tomato sauce, chiles, beans and salt. Heat thoroughly. Place in a chafing dish. Top with garnishes attractively arranged over meat mixture.

## PICKLED HOT JALAPENO DIP

Yield: 5 cups
Prep Time: 1 hour

- 1  11½ oz. jar jalapeno pepper strips
- 1  16 oz. container sour cream
- ½  tsp. salt
- ½  tsp. paprika
- ½  tsp. cumin powder
- 2  8 oz. pkgs. cream cheese, softened
   fresh parsley for garnish
   paprika
- 1  large bag corn chips

Drain jalapeno pepper strips and chop well. Combine sour cream, salt, paprika and cumin with jalapenos in a large bowl. Add cream cheese to sour cream mixture and blend until smooth. Pour into a decorative bowl and chill before serving. Garnish with fresh parsley sprigs and jalapenos and sprinkle with paprika. Serve with corn chips.

## CHILES AND DRIED BEEF DIP

Yield: 2½ cups
Prep Time: 2½ hours

- 2  T. butter
- 1  4 oz. can green chiles, chopped
- 1  4 oz. jar dried beef, diced
- 1  medium onion, minced
- 1  clove garlic, minced
- 8  oz. cream cheese, creamed
- 2  T. milk
- 4  drops Tabasco

Melt butter in a heavy skillet and add green chiles, dried beef, onion and garlic. Saute until onion is tender. In a mixing bowl, combine cream cheese and milk, blend until smooth. Add Tabasco and blend again. Chill 2 hours or until firm. Serve with crackers or chips.

## COTTAGE CHEESE AND GREEN CHILE DIP

Yield: 4½ cups
Prep Time: 2¼ hours

- 1 16 oz. container cottage cheese small curd
- 1 16 oz. container sour cream
- 1 tsp. salt
- 1 7 oz. can green chiles, drained
- ⅓ cup minced cucumbers
- ⅓ cup minced green onions
- 1 lg. pimento minced
- ½ tsp. Tabasco

Combine all ingredients and blend until creamy. Chill 2 hours before serving.

## MEXICAN HOT BEAN DIP

Yield: 4 cups
Prep Time: 2¼ hours

- 8 strips bacon
- 2 16 oz. cans refried beans
- 1 lg. onion, minced
- 1 clove garlic, minced
- 2 T. Tabasco
- 2-3 T. sour cream
  whole pickled jalapeno peppers for garnish

Fry and crumble bacon (reserve drippings). Place crumbled bacon in a 2-quart sauce pan with beans and stir well. Saute onions and garlic in bacon drippings until tender. Add to bean mixture. Add Tabasco and sour cream and blend until smooth. Chill for 1 hour. Shape into a ball and place on wax paper and chill for 1 hour. Garnish with whole pickled jalapeno peppers.

## PICO DE GALLO
## (Mexican Salsa)

    1  cup tomato, coarsely chopped
    1  cup white onion, coarsely chopped
    ½  cup cilantro, chopped
    ½  cup green chile peppers, finely chopped
       salt to taste

Mix all ingredients and enjoy. This not only spices up camp
food from eggs before dawn to warmed up soup when you
return to camp too late or too tired to cook, but is also an
excellent chip dip to keep your hungry hunting buddies sated
while you prepare your favorite wild game recipe.

**Joe Johnston**
**President**
**Hoyt/Easton**

It was 30 years ago that Joe Johnston was introduced to archery by a friend in Phoenix, Arizona. Today he is President of Hoyt/Easton, one of the most progressive companies in the bowhunting and general archery market.

Along the way, Joe has accomplished a great deal in the sport of bowhunting and has enjoyed many hunts himself. He is past-president of Arizona Bowhunters & Field Archery Association, past-director of the National Field Archery Association, founder and director of the Las Vegas Tournament, past-president, -director and -vice president of the Archery Manufacturers Organization.

Joe has taken many species of game with bow and arrow including 11 javalina.

# VENISON ROUND STEAK

Serves: 2-4
Prep Time: 2 hours

> 2 lbs. venison steaks or roast
> 1 small onion, diced
> 2 cans golden mushroom soup
> garlic salt
> celery salt
> pepper

Lightly flour both sides of meat and brown. Place in roaster,
sprinkle onion over meat. In bowl, combine soup with 2 cans of
water. Mix well and pour over meat. Bake at 375 degrees for
1½ hours. Serve with wild rice casserole.

**Ken Laird**
**President**
**American Archery**

Ken Laird spent the
majority of his years in
the trucking industry.
In 1982 he retired and
moved to his vacation
residence at Florence,
Wisconsin. For a year
and a half, Ken spent
his time putting his
farm into a reasonable
wildlife habitat, plant-
ing over 200 apple
trees and developing
a trout pond.

While farming, Ken
kept looking for a
business he could
locate in Florence, to
assist the economy of
the area. With the help of Benji Roemer and Acie Johnson, Ken
purchased the assets of American Archery at Oconto Falls,
Wisconsin, and moved into a new plant at Florence. The plant
now operates with approximately 25 people in a picturesque
north woods setting, and with as dedicated and efficient a work
force as Laird has ever been associated with.

American Archery is dedicated to producing the finest quality
product at the most reasonable cost, and wholly through a pro-
fessional dealer base. Laird has put together a fine manage-
ment team and they are very pleased with their ability to
penetrate the archery market.

## BEST OF BREAST WILD TURKEY

Serves: varies
Prep Time: 10 minutes

    **sliced wild turkey breast**
1 **egg**
¾ **cup milk**
¾ **cup flour**
    **seasonings to taste**

After thoroughly cleaning wild turkey, wrap and place in freezer. Allow 1½ to 3 hours, depending on size of bird. Check regularly to determine the stiffness of the breast. Breast should be firm enough to slice, but not frozen solid. Slice into ⅜-inch slices. Beat together the egg and milk and dip slices into mixture. Shake dipped slices in floured bag. Place in heated skillet with olive oil or vegetable oil. Quick-fry several minutes on each side until done. Excellent hot or cold.

**Frank Piper**
**President**
**Penn's Woods**
**Products**

Frank Piper is presi-
dent of Penn's Woods
Products, one of the
oldest manufacturers of
turkey calls and hunt-
ing accessories in the
United States. Penn's
Woods, originally
known as the Tom
Turpin Company, dates
back to the earliest
days of the sport of wild
turkey hunting. Its
product quality and
support of the wild
turkey resource has
enabled many hunters
to take advantage of
this recipe. Piper said,
"It is our sincere hope that by using Penn's Woods calls and
accessories, you too will be able to enjoy Best of Breast Wild
Turkey."

# DESCHUTES APPLE PAN DOUDIE

Serves: 4
Prep Time: 45 minutes

2 lg. Granny Smith apples
buttermilk baking mix
1 pint whipping cream
¼ lb. butter

2 tsp. cinnamon
¾ cup milk
1 egg

Preheat 5-quart cast iron Dutch oven over campfire for 10 minutes. Place 2 T. butter in oven. Add diced apple and allow to simmer for 5 minutes. While apples are simmering, mix 2 cups buttermilk mix with ¾ cup milk, 1 egg and 2 tsp. cinnamon. Add this mixture to oven. Cover oven and place coals on top and bottom for 20 minutes. Watch for even cooking. Whip cream and place on top of hot Pan Doudie.

**Tim Boyle**
**General Manager**
**Columbia Sportswear**

Tim Boyle grew up with
the business his grand-
father started nearly
half a century ago.
Today, Tim is general
manager of Columbia
Sportswear, one of the
largest sportswear
companies in the
Northwest.

Paul Lamfrom, Tim's
grandfather, purchased
Columbia Sportswear
in 1937. Lamfrom had
owned the largest shirt
company in Germany
and the expertise that
he had gained in ap-
parel manufacturing
was passed on to his family. Today the company is headed by
Lamfrom's daughter, Gert Boyle, and her son, Tim.

Columbia has emerged as an industry leader. Aggressive
research and development, unparalleled product innovation
and strict quality control are the major factors that have con-
tributed to the company's growth in the past, and will continue
to be of utmost importance in the future.

When Tim is not at the reigns of Columbia Sportswear, he can
often be found knee-deep in the Deschutes River, casting for
Rainbow Trout, or in a duck blind.

## QUAIL WITH HERBS

Serves: 2-3
Prep Time: 45 minutes

    4 quail
    4 chicken livers
    3 T. butter
    ½ tsp. thyme
    ½ tsp. rosemary
       salt and pepper
    2 T. butter, melted
    4 strips bacon

Saute chicken livers in butter until golden brown. Remove from
heat and stir in thyme, rosemary, salt and pepper. Stuff each
quail with a chicken liver and a spoonful of butter sauce. Tie
legs close to the body. Brush quail with melted butter and place
bacon over breast and thighs. Roast at 450 degrees for about 20
minutes or until done. Serve quail on a toasted slice of french
bread. Surround with mushrooms sauteed in butter, garlic and
minced scallions.

**Frank Kenna
President
The Marlin Firearms
Company**

Frank Kenna is the president of The Marlin Firearms Company in North Haven, Connecticut. Marlin manufactures sporting rifles and shotguns, and is the largest producer of rifles in the United States, with a worldwide distribution.

Mr. Kenna assumed the position of president of the company in 1959, following the death of his brother, Roger. Rapid growth of the business soon required larger quarters, and a new plant was built in North Haven, where the manufacturing facility was moved in 1969, together with the Industrial Division.

## PAN FRIED TURKEY BREAST

Serves: varies
Prep Time: 10 minutes

**thin sliced strips of fileted turkey breast**
**flour**
**salt and pepper**
**granulated garlic**
**milk**
**oil**

Mix flour, salt, pepper and garlic to taste. Wash strips of breast in cool water and dredge in flour. Dip floured strips in milk, then flour again. Drop strips into hot oil. Fry until golden brown, turning if necessary.

**Wilbur Primos**
**President**
**Primos Yelpers**

Wilbur Primos grew up hunting turkeys, and was infatuated by their language. In his early days of hunting, Wilber used a box call, but realized that something was missing. As he listened to more and more turkeys, he understood that turkeys were just like people; some have high voices, some low voices and some coarse voices. It was then that he decided to produce a call that would reproduce all of the sounds of the wild turkey.

Needing a day-by-day contact with wild turkeys so that he could record their sounds year round, he acquired four hens and two gobblers, and affectionately named a pair Loretta (shown above) and Conway. It was a real treat to Wilbur to have a wild turkey voicing her vocabulary not 18 inches from his face, and after several years of studying and recording them, he developed his first turkey call, the True Triple.

One thing led to another, and Wilbur found it too difficult to make the 500 or so calls he was making each year for friends and local sporting good stores, so he had some equipment built, making it easier to make the parts he needed for the calls.

Primos Yelpers calls are put together by hand. They stand behind their products, guaranteeing that if for any reason one of their products does not perform due to manufacturing defects, they will replace it.

## SAUTEED VENISON OR TURKEY

Serves: 2-4
Prep Time: 10 minutes

> **2 lbs. venison tenderloin or turkey breast**
> **1 stick of butter**
> **salt**
> **lemon pepper (key ingredient)**

Slice meat ¼-inch thick. Sprinkle each slice with salt and lemon pepper. Melt butter in skillet, keeping heat low enough so that butter does not burn. Saute meat slices in butter about 2 minutes on each side. Serve hot as main course and as sandwiches the following day.

**Jim Crumley**
**President**
**Bowing Enterprises Inc.**

Jim Crumley is founder
and president of Bow-
ing Enterprises, Inc.,
and originator of the
Trebark Camouflage
design. He was a
public school teacher,
administrator and hunt-
ing guide before start-
ing his company in
1980. His favorite pur-
suits are fall bowhunt-
ing and spring gobbler
hunting, with a pinch
of dove shooting, duck
hunting and trout
fishing thrown in.

# CANADA GOOSE SANDWICH SPREAD

| | | | |
|---|---|---|---|
| 1 | Canada goose | 2 | hard boiled eggs |
| 2 | chicken bouillon cubes | 1 | medium dill pickle |
| 1 | tsp. parsley | 1 | stalk celery |
| ½ | tsp. pepper | 1 | cup mayonnaise |
| 1 | small onion, chopped | ¼ | cup dill pickle juice |
| 2 | T. barbeque sauce | ¼ | cup prepared mustard |

Place goose in large pan. Cover with cold water to which has been added the bouillon cubes, parsley, pepper and onion. Cover with tight fitting lid and boil slowly until tender. Take from heat and let cool in broth while still covered. Remove meat from bone and chop or grind into large bowl. Mix thoroughly with the mayonnaise, barbeque sauce, chopped celery, pickles, eggs, juice and mustard. Store in covered plastic or glass container. Serve as needed. Will keep for a few days in refrigerator or freezes for 2 weeks without loss of flavor.

**Bruce Hodgdon**
**Founder**
**Hodgdon Powder**
**Co. Inc.**

In 1952 Bruce Hodgdon quit his job with the local gas company to start a full-time gun powder business. He had three employees at that time—his wife and two young sons. Today, Hodgdon Powder is still a family owned business that is in touch with the shooting public. Hodgdon's offers 16 different burning rates of specialized powders and three grades of Pyrodex, the replica black powder.

Bruce's favorite pasttime is shooting prairie dogs and when the occasion presents itself, spending a couple of days at his goose blind in north central Missouri.

In 1982, the National Rifle Association recognized the contributions that Bruce Hodgdon has made to the shooting sports by awarding him their prestigious Public Service Award.

## THE BILL HARPER SPECIAL

Serves: 4
Prep Time: 1 hour

```
    2  lbs. venison, cubed
 1½  cups celery stalks and tops, chopped
    1  medium onion, chopped
   ½  lb. fresh mushrooms, sliced
   ½  green pepper, chopped
    1  T. Worcestershire
   ¼  tsp. allspice
   ½  tsp. garlic powder
   ¼  tsp. paprika
   ½  cup wine
    2  cans cream of chicken soup
    8  oz. milk or
   ½  pint sour cream
```

Brown meat in butter and simmer until tender. Add vegetables
and seasonings. Saute until tender. Add wine, soup and the
milk or sour cream. Heat through and serve over wild rice,
white rice or noodles.

## Bill Harper
## President
## Lohman Manufacturing Company

Bill Harper, well-known sportsman, game calling expert, and president of Lohman Manufacturing Company, Inc., is always working to improve and develop new game calls and accessories. Lohman has produced calls of the finest quality since 1937.

Today, this company is the innovator of the game call industry, through Bill's actual hunting experiences and continuing research.

# GERMAN VENISON STEW
## with Black Forest Mushrooms and Spaetzle

Serves: varies
Prep Time: 1½ hours

|  |  |  |  |
|---|---|---|---|
| | venison shoulder meat | | black forest mushrooms |
| | bacon | 1 | lb. flour |
| | butter | 3 | eggs |
| | onion | 1 | cup water |
| 1 | cup beef broth | | grated cheese |
| | peppercorns | | |
| ½ | bay leaf | | |
| 3 | T. red burgundy wine | | |

Cut well-aged shoulder meat into ½-inch pieces. Roll in flour and panfry with bacon pieces, butter and 1 diced onion until golden brown. Add salt, beef broth, whole peppercorns, bay leaf. Cover and simmer for 15 to 20 minutes. Thicken gravy with flour and wine before serving.

Saute mushrooms with bacon bits, diced onion, butter and salt. Garnish with parsley.

Spaetzle: Mix 1 lb. flour, 3 eggs, salt, 1 cup water, grated cheese and browned butter. Blend well, adding flour slowly until slightly foamy. Let sit 30 minutes. Heat 2 pots of saltwater and bring one pot to a boil. Press dough through sieve or pastamaker to form small lumps which drop into boiling water. When they rise to the top they are done. Transfer to other pot with non-boiling water until serving to keep hot. You can brown some onions in butter and pour over the Spaetzle when serving.

**Wolfgang Harms**
**President**
**Pioneer & Co.**

Wolfgang Harms is
president of Pioneer &
Company, the U.S
Marketing Office for
Steiner Military/Marine
binoculars, which are
the finest, precision-
made German optics.
Steiner Military
Binoculars have
penetrating light power
that literally illuminate
the shade under trees
in dawn and dusk.

# FAJITAS DE GANZA AND TACOS AL CARBON

Prep Time: 1½ hours

> **breasts of geese**
> **seasoned salt**
> **pepper**
> **soy sauce**
> 1 **lime or lemon per whole breast**
> 2 **lg. yellow onions**
> 2-3 **lg. tomatoes**
> 2 **jalapenos**
> 1 **pkg. tortillas**

Slice partially through breasts across the grain, making each cut ½-inch wide. Squeeze lemon or lime on meat and salt and pepper. Slice onion to cover breasts and cover with soy sauce. Marinate for 1 hour. While the meat is marinating, chop finely the tomatoes, onion and jalapenos. Fire should be hot (coals, not flames), about 6 to 10 inches from meat. While grilling the meat, cook the marinade also. It makes a delicious gravy. The cooked onions are super. Serve as you would any steak with the cooked onions as a vegetable and the tomatoes and onions as a great tasting garnish.

To make tacos, dice fajita and, on a hot tortilla, put a handful of diced meat, some onion, tomato and jalapeno garnish. Roll up taco and enjoy this South Texas treat. Deer, ducks and doves are good this way also.

**Charles Barry
President
Texas Hunting
Products**

Chuck Barry, president of Texas Hunting Products, is an avid goose hunter. He emphasizes two words in the description of his equipment—function and durability. Based on his own experiences and frustrations, he knows the feelings of anger that occur at four o'clock in the morning when you are wading or hiking towards your favorite spot to hunt and your equipment fails you. His equipment does what it is designed to do for a long, long time. Some of his products include: The Duck Strap/Gun Strap, a bird sling that will not rot or mildew but will carry your shotgun, Decoy Bags that last longer than your decoys, and Goose Rags, 100 of which weigh only four pounds and are effective as full bodies.

# SEND US YOUR GAME RECIPE

**Title:** _____

**Serves:** _____

**Prep Time:** _____

## Ingredients:

_____
_____
_____
_____
_____
_____
_____
_____
_____

## Directions:

_____  fold here
_____
_____
_____
_____
_____
_____
_____
_____
_____
_____
_____
_____
_____
_____
_____
_____
_____
_____
_____

Your NAHC Member # _____

Your Name _____

Address _____

City/State/Zip _____

**North American Hunting Club**
**P. O. Box 35557**
**Minneapolis, MN 55435**

# Hunters belong in the NAHC...
## and it's so *simple* to join!
### *Cut out and mail one of the cards below.*

---

**Count me in...**
**I want to increase my hunting pleasure and skill.**
Here's my $18 annual dues for membership in the North American Hunting Club Inc. I understand my membership will start immediately upon receipt of this application and continue for 12 months.

RECOMMENDED BY

Name _____

NAHC MEMBER # _____

Name _____

Address _____

City _____ State _____ Zip _____

Type of Hunter: ☐ Firearms ☐ Archery ☐ Handgun ☐ Muzzleloader

Check Game Hunted: ☐ Big Game ☐ Small Game ☐ Waterfowl ☐ Upland Birds

*Check One:*
☐ Check enclosed
☐ Bill my MasterCard
☐ Bill my VISA
☐ Bill me later

Credit Card No. _____ Exp. Date _____

Signature _____

---

**Count me in...**
**I want to increase my hunting pleasure and skill.**
Here's my $18 annual dues for membership in the North American Hunting Club Inc. I understand my membership will start immediately upon receipt of this application and continue for 12 months.

RECOMMENDED BY

Name _____

NAHC MEMBER # _____

Name _____

Address _____

City _____ State _____ Zip _____

Type of Hunter: ☐ Firearms ☐ Archery ☐ Handgun ☐ Muzzleloader

Check Game Hunted: ☐ Big Game ☐ Small Game ☐ Waterfowl ☐ Upland Birds

*Check One:*
☐ Check enclosed
☐ Bill my MasterCard
☐ Bill my VISA
☐ Bill me later

Credit Card No. _____ Exp. Date _____

Signature _____

## BUSINESS REPLY CARD
FIRST CLASS      PERMIT NO. 17619     MPLS., MN

POSTAGE WILL BE PAID BY ADDRESSEE

North American Hunting Club, Inc.
P.O. Box 35557
Minneapolis, Minn. 55435

NO POSTAGE
NECESSARY
IF MAILED
IN THE
UNITED STATES

## BUSINESS REPLY CARD
FIRST CLASS      PERMIT NO. 17619     MPLS., MN

POSTAGE WILL BE PAID BY ADDRESSEE

North American Hunting Club, Inc.
P.O. Box 35557
Minneapolis, Minn. 55435

NO POSTAGE
NECESSARY
IF MAILED
IN THE
UNITED STATES

## ALLIGATOR
fried, 115
meatballs, 115

## ANTELOPE
steaks, 109

## BEAR
ribs, 112
roast, 112
spaghetti, 111
stroganoff, 113

## BEAVER
tail w/beans, 26

## BREADS
baking powder biscuits, 10
bannock, 12
beer pan, 153
cornbread, 13, 152
corn fritters, 12
Dutch oven biscuits, 11
empanadas, 150
fried bread, 16
gingerbread puffs, 15
griddle cakes, 152
Indian pie, 16
muffins, 13
sopapillas, 151
yeast biscuits, 9

## BUFFALO
hump roast, 63

## CARIBOU
braised, 54
curried, 53
foil lunch, 56
steak, 54
stew, 55, 56

## CHILI
50,000 watt, 142
Australian, 131
baked, 147
beans and rice, 149
Boston, 127
buffalo, 137
buzzard's breath, 140
cactus, 141
California, 134
chocolate, 146
Cincinnati, 128
Colorado, 130
Perry Como's, 123
Ken Curtis', 124
Dante's inferno armadillo, 144
Diamondback, 138
eye-opener, 145
James Garner's, 126
general alarm, 139
Goober Pea, 132
Janet Guthrie's, 122
Carol Hancock's, 121
Italian, 135
Lady Bird Johnson's, 125
macaroni, 148
oriental, 133
sausalito, 143
sheepherder's, 136
Texas Red, 129
vegetable, 127

## COUGAR
you won't believe it's, 61

## COYOTE
soup, 116

## DESSERTS
apple marshmallow, 70

apple pan doudie, 168
blueberries, 73, 74
boiled cake, 76
caramel sauce, 75
carrot pudding, 75
chocolate crazy cake, 71
coconut, 70
dates, 74

**DUCK**
breast fry, 69
currant, 82
in orange sauce, 81
teal in wine sauce, 83

**ELK**
hobo packs, 51
pot roast, 33
shish kabob, 52
tacos, 31
teriyaki steak, 34

**GOOSE**
Canada, 176
fajitas and tacos, 182

**GROUSE**
blue, with rice, 67
foiled game birds, 87
smothered bird, 87
wild, 86

**HINTS,** 8, 14, 30, 68, 72

**JAVELINA**
wrap-ups, 28

**LION**
loin, 62
ribs, 114

**MISCELLANEOUS**
dumplings, 49, 55, 90
holupchi, 26
Pemmican, 17
porcupine and pineapple, 114
refried bean pie, 153
sausage and peppers, 64
small game enchiladas, 91

**MOOSE**
burgundy, 59
dinner in foil, 60
loaf, 58, 110
nose, 60
stroganoff, 57

**PHEASANT**
cacciatore, 79
cordon bleu, 80
corn chowder, 78

**PTARMIGAN**
pie, 84

**QUAIL**
curried, 84
with herbs, 170

**RABBIT**
beer braised, 65
cookout, 66
meatloaf, 89
saute, 88
stew, 88

**SAUCES & DIPS**
chiled sour cream, 155
chiles and dried beef dip, 159
cottage cheese and
    green chile, 160

guacamole, 154
Mexican hot bean, 160
Mexican salad dressing, 157
mustard-chili salsa, 156
pickled hot jalapeno dip, 159
Pico de Gallo, 162
red chili sauce, 155
sombrero chili dip, 158

## SQUIRREL
meatloaf, 89
stew, 90

## TURKEY
breast, 166, 172
sauteed, 174
tidbits, 85

## VENISON
backstraps, 48
barbeque, 103, 104
Bill Harper special, 178
braised, 39
buckaroo dinner, 46
bundles to go, 43
burgers, 50
casserole, 102
cheeseburger pie, 95
chili, 35
chops, 100
cook-out, 18
curried rice and meat, 27
with egg noodles, 42
Eugene, 100
filet mignon, 45
goulash, 46
hamburgers in a can, 24
Hawaiian, 47

Italian rolls, 94
jerky, 29, 108
macaroni meal, 23
marinated, 97
meatballs, 92, 104
meatloaf, 96
minestrone dinner, 25
one-pot meal, 24
pit-fire roast, 37
pot roast, 36
quick meal, 18
with rice, 105
salami, 107
Saskatchewan, 99
sausage, 106
sauteed, 174
scallopini, 97
shepherd's pie, 40
sloppies, 29
soup, 21
spaghetti, 92, 93
steaks, 44, 45, 96, 98, 164
stew, 20, 22, 35, 38, 39,
    40, 49, 101, 180
stroganoff, 32
tenderloins, 41
trail sandwich, 19